Linux Troubleshooting Mastery:

Diagnosing and Resolving System Issues

Sarful Hassan

Preface

This book, *Linux Troubleshooting Mastery: Diagnosing and Resolving System Issues*, is a comprehensive guide designed to empower readers to tackle a wide range of Linux system issues with confidence. Whether you're a seasoned administrator or a curious beginner, this book provides the tools, techniques, and insights you need to become proficient in diagnosing and resolving Linux problems effectively.

Who This Book Is For This book is for:

- System administrators and engineers who want to improve their Linux troubleshooting skills.
- IT professionals responsible for maintaining Linux-based environments.
- Developers seeking to understand the inner workings of Linux systems for debugging purposes.
- Enthusiasts and learners eager to gain deeper insights into Linux operations.

How This Book Is Organized The book is divided into 16 chapters, starting with foundational concepts and progressively moving toward advanced topics:

- Chapters 1–3 introduce troubleshooting methodologies and tools.
- Chapters 4–9 address specific issues related to booting, filesystems, memory, networking, applications, and the kernel.
- Chapters 10–16 delve into specialized areas such as security, storage, performance, and virtualization.

What Was Left Out This book focuses solely on Linux troubleshooting techniques. Topics such as general Linux administration, command-line basics, and comprehensive system performance tuning are only touched upon when directly relevant to troubleshooting.

Code Style (About the Code) All examples in this book use a consistent, readable coding style. Code snippets are formatted for clarity and include comments where necessary. Unless stated otherwise, examples assume a bash shell and root-level access.

Release Notes This edition reflects the latest updates in Linux distributions as of January 2025, incorporating new troubleshooting tools and methodologies. Future editions will address evolving trends and technologies in the Linux ecosystem.

Notes on the First Edition This first edition of *Linux Troubleshooting Mastery* aims to establish a foundation for readers to approach Linux system issues methodically. Constructive feedback is welcome to refine and enhance subsequent editions.

MechatronicsLAB Online Learning

MechatronicsLAB is committed to providing high-quality learning resources for technology enthusiasts. Visit us online to access:

- Supplemental materials for this book.
- Online courses and tutorials.
- Forums for discussion and support.

Contact Us Email: mechatronicslab@gmail.com
Website: mechatronicslab.net

Acknowledgments for the First Edition This book would not have been possible without the support and expertise of countless individuals. I extend my gratitude to my colleagues, reviewers, and the Linux community for their invaluable contributions.

Disclaimer The information provided in this book is for educational purposes only. While every effort has been made to ensure accuracy, the author and publisher are not responsible for errors, omissions, or damages resulting from the use of the information herein.

Table of Contents

Chapter 1: Introduction to Linux Troubleshooting

In this chapter, we introduce Linux troubleshooting and explain why it's a critical skill for anyone using or managing a Linux system. You'll learn what troubleshooting is, the types of problems that can occur in Linux, and the tools that can help you resolve these issues. Additionally, we'll cover proactive and reactive troubleshooting and explain how proper documentation can make resolving problems more efficient.

Why Troubleshooting Skills Matter

Troubleshooting is the process of identifying and fixing problems when they occur. Imagine you're working on your computer, and suddenly, a program freezes. You click on it, but nothing happens. Troubleshooting is the process you use to figure out why the program froze and fix it.

Why It's Essential for Linux Systems

1. **Widespread Use:** Linux powers servers, desktops, and embedded devices worldwide.
2. **Critical Systems:** Many websites and applications rely on Linux. If something goes wrong, it can lead to significant downtime or crashes.
3. **Quick Recovery:** Troubleshooting allows you to find the root cause of an issue and resolve it quickly to restore system functionality.
   Without troubleshooting skills, issues could remain unresolved for extended periods, disrupting productivity and causing frustration. Effective troubleshooting saves time and ensures systems run smoothly.

The Role of Troubleshooting in System Administration

A System Administrator (SysAdmin) is responsible for maintaining and managing computer systems. For SysAdmins who work with Linux, troubleshooting is one of their most critical skills.

Responsibilities in Troubleshooting

1. **Identify the Issue:** Determine what is causing the problem.
2. **Analyze the Cause:** Pinpoint whether it's a hardware, software, or network issue.
3. **Apply a Fix:** Resolve the problem as quickly and efficiently as possible.

   Example: Imagine a server hosting an online store crashes. A SysAdmin must diagnose the issue, such as a software bug, hardware failure, or network problem, and resolve it to minimize downtime.

Importance of Reducing Downtime

Downtime refers to periods when a system or application is unavailable. Minimizing downtime is crucial for maintaining productivity and ensuring user satisfaction.

Impact of Downtime

- **For Businesses:** Lost sales and reduced customer trust if websites or applications go offline.
- **For Teams:** Disruptions in communication and workflow if critical tools are unavailable.

Role of Troubleshooting

- **Fast Resolution:** The faster you identify and fix issues, the less impact downtime has.
- **Preventative Measures:** Effective troubleshooting helps identify weak points, reducing the likelihood of future issues.

Common Challenges in Linux Systems

Linux systems are robust, but they can encounter several challenges. Let's explore some common problems:

Hardware Failures

Hardware issues involve physical components such as hard drives, memory (RAM), CPUs, or power supplies. Symptoms include:

- **Crashes:** The system suddenly stops working.
- **Startup Issues:** The operating system fails to load.

  Example: If a hard drive fails, you might lose access to important files. In such cases, replacing the faulty hardware is often the solution.

Software Bugs and Misconfigurations

- **Bugs:** Errors in code causing programs to crash or behave unexpectedly.
- **Misconfigurations:** Incorrect settings that prevent software from functioning properly.

  Example: Updating a misconfigured program or fixing its settings can resolve issues such as slow performance or failure to start.

Network Latency and Connectivity Issues

Problems with internet or network connections can cause delays or prevent communication entirely.

- **Latency:** Delays in data transfer between systems.
- **Connectivity Issues:** Inability to connect to the internet or other devices.

  Example: If you can't access a website, troubleshooting might involve checking network cables, restarting the router, or adjusting system settings.

Tools and Techniques for Effective Troubleshooting

Linux offers several tools for diagnosing and resolving issues. Here are some essential tools:

dmesg

- **Function:** Displays system messages, particularly useful for diagnosing hardware issues.
- **Example:** If a hard drive isn't working, dmesg might show errors like "Hard drive failure."

top

- **Function:** Displays real-time information about CPU and memory usage.
- **Example:** If your system is slow, use top to identify programs consuming excessive resources.

ping

- **Function:** Checks connectivity between your system and another device or server.
- **Example:** Use ping to test whether your computer can reach a specific website or server.

These tools are simple to use and provide valuable insights into system health.

Proactive vs. Reactive Troubleshooting

Proactive Troubleshooting

- **Definition:** Preventing problems before they occur by regularly monitoring and maintaining the system.
- **Example:** Setting up automatic updates to ensure your software stays secure and up-to-date.

Reactive Troubleshooting

- **Definition:** Responding to and fixing problems after they occur.
- **Example:** Diagnosing a server crash using tools like top or ping to identify the root cause.

Best Practice: Combine proactive and reactive troubleshooting to minimize issues while being prepared to address them when they arise.

The Role of Documentation in Problem Resolution

Why Documentation is Important

1. **Efficiency:** Documenting past issues and their solutions allows for faster resolution if the problem recurs.
2. **Collaboration:** Helps others on your team troubleshoot similar issues.

What to Document

- **Problem Details:** What was happening when the issue occurred.
- **Resolution Steps:** Actions taken to resolve the problem.
- **Additional Notes:** Any observations or settings that could help in the future.

    Example: If a software application frequently crashes, documenting the fix (e.g., updating to a stable version) helps resolve future occurrences quickly.

1.8 Conclusion

In this chapter, you learned:

- The importance of troubleshooting in Linux systems.
- Common problems like hardware failures, software bugs, and network issues.
- Essential tools such as dmesg, top, and ping.
- The difference between proactive and reactive troubleshooting.
- How documentation can make troubleshooting easier and more efficient.
    In the next chapter, we'll explore specific steps and methods for diagnosing and resolving Linux system issues in detail.

Chapter 2: Troubleshooting Methodologies

This chapter explains how to solve problems step by step. You'll learn how to identify symptoms, determine the root cause of issues, and prioritize the most critical problems to address. We'll also cover how to use checklists, logs, and documentation to stay organized. Finally, we'll explore different troubleshooting approaches, such as Divide-and-Conquer and Bottom-Up, and discuss the importance of gathering user feedback during the troubleshooting process.

Understanding the Problem-Solving Process

Troubleshooting is the process of identifying and fixing problems. Think of it as solving a puzzle:

1. **Identify the problem:** What isn't working? Is the computer slow? Does the program keep crashing?
2. **Find the cause:** Why is this happening? Is the hardware faulty? Is there a bug in the software?
3. **Fix the problem:** Once you understand the cause, apply a solution.
4. **Test the fix:** Verify that the solution resolves the issue and prevents it from recurring.

This structured approach ensures issues are addressed methodically and effectively.

Identifying Symptoms and Root Causes
Symptoms
Symptoms are the signs that indicate something is wrong. They help you notice the problem but don't explain why it happened.
- **Example:** If a computer's screen goes blank, that's a symptom.
- **Example:** A program freezing repeatedly is another symptom.

Root Cause

The root cause is the underlying reason the problem occurred. Fixing it ensures the symptoms don't return.

- **Example:** A blank screen might result from a broken cable, and replacing it resolves the issue.
- **Example:** A freezing program might be caused by a bug in the software, which can be fixed by updating the application.

Key Point: While symptoms highlight the issue, the root cause is what you need to address to resolve the problem effectively.

Prioritizing Critical Issues

Not all issues have the same level of urgency. Some problems must be fixed immediately, while others can wait.

- **Urgent:** A server crash during peak business hours requires immediate attention.
- **Non-Urgent:** A minor delay in loading a non-critical application can be addressed later.

Why Prioritization Matters

Focusing on the most pressing issues ensures that critical systems remain operational and downtime is minimized.

Creating a Troubleshooting Checklist

A checklist ensures a systematic approach to resolving problems and prevents you from missing important steps.

Example Checklist: Computer Won't Turn On

1. **Check the power cable:** Ensure it's plugged in and the power button is on.
2. **Verify the power supply:** Check if the computer's lights or fans are working.
3. **Inspect the screen:** Ensure the monitor is powered on and connected properly.
4. **Listen for sounds:** Check for fan noise or hard drive activity.
5. **Test another outlet:** Try a different power source to rule out electrical issues.

Using a checklist helps you work methodically and improves the efficiency of your troubleshooting process.

Systematic Steps for Resolution

Follow a logical order to troubleshoot issues effectively. For example, to resolve a slow computer:

1. **Check for updates:** Ensure the operating system and software are current.
2. **Analyze resource usage:** Use tools like top to identify memory or CPU-intensive processes.
3. **Check disk space:** Verify that sufficient storage is available.
4. **Close unnecessary programs:** Shut down non-essential applications to free resources.
5. **Restart the computer:** A reboot often resolves temporary glitches.

   Pro Tip: Treat troubleshooting like following a recipe—stick to the steps to avoid missing critical details.

Escalation Points and Team Collaboration

When to Escalate

1. **Exhausted Options:** You've tried all basic troubleshooting steps without success.
2. **Beyond Your Expertise:** The issue requires specialized knowledge, such as advanced network diagnostics or programming fixes.

Importance of Collaboration

1. **Hardware Issues:** Involve hardware specialists if physical components fail.
2. **Software Bugs:** Collaborate with developers for code-related problems.

   Example: If you encounter a persistent bug, sharing logs and documentation with your team can expedite resolution.

Using Logs and Documentation

Leveraging System Logs

Linux systems store logs that act as a "diary" of events, helping diagnose issues:

- **/var/log/**: Contains system logs for troubleshooting.
- **journalctl**: Displays detailed event histories.

Example: Use journalctl to review error messages after a program crashes. This can provide insight into what caused the issue.

Maintaining a Troubleshooting Log

Documenting your troubleshooting steps creates a reference for future issues.

Log Template:

- **Problem:** Describe the issue.
- **Steps Taken:** Record actions you've tried.
- **Solution:** Note how the problem was resolved.
- **Date:** Include when the problem occurred.

Example:

- **Problem:** Software crashes on startup.
- **Steps Taken:** Restarted, reinstalled, checked logs.
- **Solution:** Applied a patch provided by the developer.
- **Date:** January 15, 2025.

Approaches to Troubleshooting

Divide-and-Conquer

Break the problem into smaller parts to isolate the issue:

1. Check the server.
2. Verify network connectivity.
3. Inspect the application.

Bottom-Up

Start with basic components (hardware, power) and move upwards to software and configurations:

- **Step 1:** Ensure cables and power supplies are functional.
- **Step 2:** Check operating system boot logs.
- **Step 3:** Analyze running applications.

Top-Down

Begin with high-level components (applications, software) and work down:

- **Step 1:** Check if the application is running.
- **Step 2:** Verify network settings.
- **Step 3:** Inspect hardware for issues.

  Choose an approach based on the nature of the problem for faster resolution.

Importance of User Feedback in Diagnosing Issues

Why Feedback Matters

1. **Clues:** Users can describe symptoms you may not notice.
2. **Prioritization:** Users can identify which issues are most disruptive.

Example:

- If multiple users report slow website performance, check server load or network bandwidth.
- If a single user experiences software crashes, focus on their configuration.

  Pro Tip: Actively listen to users and ask clarifying questions to gather actionable insights.

Conclusion

Key Takeaways

- **Problem-Solving Process:** Identify, analyze, fix, and verify issues systematically.
- **Symptoms vs. Root Causes:** Understand the difference and focus on resolving root causes.
- **Prioritization:** Address the most critical issues first.
- **Checklists and Documentation:** Use structured methods to stay organized and efficient.
- **Collaboration and Logs:** Leverage team expertise and maintain accurate records to improve troubleshooting.
- **User Feedback:** Integrate user insights to diagnose and resolve issues effectively.

In the next chapter, we will explore deeper troubleshooting techniques for Linux systems, including advanced tools and scenarios.

Chapter 3: Tools for Linux Troubleshooting

Introduction: Troubleshooting tools are essential for diagnosing and fixing common Linux issues. This chapter explains their purpose, functionality, and real-life applications in system management. By the end, you'll understand various tools and how to use them effectively.

> **Note:** Effective troubleshooting requires not just tools but also a clear understanding of how to interpret the results and act on them. Combining multiple tools often yields better outcomes.

> **Warning:** Using troubleshooting tools on production systems without preparation can lead to disruptions. Always test commands in a safe environment when possible.

The Role of Tools in Troubleshooting

- **Purpose of Tools:** These tools identify problems, analyze performance, and diagnose errors, simplifying troubleshooting and reducing downtime.
- **Key Tasks:**
  - Monitoring system health to detect anomalies.
  - Analyzing system logs to pinpoint issues.
  - Tracking disk usage to identify resource-heavy files.
  - Checking network connectivity to resolve problems.
  - Debugging programs to fix crashes or inefficiencies.
- **Definition:** A troubleshooting tool is a program or command designed to help IT professionals identify and resolve system issues efficiently.

Key Characteristics of Troubleshooting Tools

- **Real-Time Monitoring:** Tools like top and htop display current system performance, highlighting resource bottlenecks.
- **Log Analysis:** Tools like grep and Logwatch help filter and summarize logs to find relevant information quickly.

- **Debugging and Analysis:** Tools like `strace` and gdb delve into program-level issues for detailed insights.
- **Efficiency:** Tools like `iotop` streamline processes by identifying disk-intensive tasks.
- **Flexibility:** Versatile tools like Wireshark handle a variety of network-related issues.

Best Practice: Use a combination of monitoring, logging, and debugging tools for comprehensive troubleshooting. Keep a list of frequently used commands for quick reference.

System Monitoring Tools

Tool	Purpose	Example Command
top	Displays processes and resource usage	top
htop	Interactive version of top	htop
iotop	Monitors disk I/O activity	sudo iotop
glances	Provides a comprehensive system view	glances

- **Example:** Use top to identify a high-CPU process causing slowdowns and terminate it if necessary.

Log Analysis Tools

Tool	Purpose	Example Command
grep	Searches logs for specific terms	grep "error" /var/log/syslog
awk	Extracts and processes log file columns	awk '{print $1}' /var/log/syslog
sed	Modifies log entries directly	sed 's/error/warning/' logfile
Logwatch	Summarizes log files	logwatch --detail High
Kibana	Visualizes logs in a web interface	Configured via ELK stack

Warning: Modifying log files directly with sed can lead to data loss. Always create backups before editing critical logs.

Debugging Tools

- **strace:**
  - Monitors system calls made by a program to identify faulty behavior.

Example Command:
```
strace -o output.log ./my_program
```

- **ltrace:**
  - Tracks library calls to diagnose dependency issues.

Example Command:
```
ltrace ./my_program
```

- **gdb:**
  - Debugs programs by stepping through their execution.

Example Command:

```
gdb ./my_program
```

Note: Debugging tools can generate a lot of output. Use filters or redirection to make the data manageable.

Network Analysis Tools

Tool	Purpose	Example Command
ping	Tests connectivity to a host	ping 8.8.8.8
netstat	Displays active network connections	netstat -tuln
tcpdump	Captures network traffic	sudo tcpdump -i eth0
Wireshark	Visualizes and analyzes captured traffic	GUI or CLI tool setup required

Warning: Capturing live traffic with tools like tcpdump or Wireshark may expose sensitive information. Use on secure networks only.

Real-Life Troubleshooting Example

Scenario: Application Failure Due to Disk Full

1. **Identify Problem:**
   o Run df -h to check disk space. Result: /var partition is full.
2. **Locate Culprit Files:**
   o Run du -sh /var/* to identify large directories. Result: Logs in /var/log consume excessive space.

3. **Resolve Issue:**

Delete old logs with:

```
sudo find /var/log -type f -mtime +30 -delete
```

4. **Verify Resolution:**
   o Run df −h again to ensure sufficient free space.
   Best Practice: Automate log rotation using logrotate to prevent similar issues.

Checklist: Common Troubleshooting Pitfalls

1. **Skipping Basic Checks:**
   o Always start with df and du to assess disk space usage.
2. **Ignoring Logs:**
   o Analyze /var/log for errors using grep or visualization tools.
3. **Running Commands Without Testing:**
   o Test new commands on non-critical systems to avoid accidental data loss.
4. **Overlooking Dependencies:**
   o Use ltrace to diagnose library-related issues.

Simplified Commands Quick Reference

Task	Simplified Command
Check disk space	df −h
Find large directories	du −sh /path/to/directory
Repair file system	sudo fsck /dev/sda1
Search logs for errors	grep "error" /var/log/syslog
Capture network traffic	sudo tcpdump −i eth0

Practice Section

- **Exercises:**
    - Use htop to identify and terminate a resource-heavy process.
    - Use grep to locate an error in /var/log/syslog and resolve it.
    - Use df and du to analyze disk usage and free up space.
    - Capture network traffic with tcpdump and analyze it with Wireshark.
- **Troubleshooting Challenge:**
    - Scenario: Your system is experiencing high disk and network usage. Combine tools like iotop, df, and tcpdump to diagnose and resolve the problem.

Summary and Glossary

- **Key Takeaways:**
    - Troubleshooting is an iterative process that benefits from combining multiple tools.
    - Regular monitoring, log analysis, and debugging practices are essential for system reliability.
- **Glossary:**
    - **System Call:** A request by a program to the operating system for a service.
    - **Disk I/O:** Input/output operations related to a storage device.
    - **Log Rotation:** Automatically archiving and clearing old log files.
    - **Packet:** A unit of data transmitted over a network.

Chapter 4: Troubleshooting Boot Issues

Introduction: Understanding and troubleshooting boot issues in Linux is crucial for maintaining system availability. This chapter explores the boot process, common issues, and tools to diagnose and resolve boot-related problems.

- **Purpose:** Equip beginners with the knowledge to comprehend and troubleshoot the Linux boot process effectively.
- **Real-life Application:** Boot issues are critical as they can prevent system access. The chapter covers tools and methods to diagnose and resolve these failures.

Note: Troubleshooting boot issues often requires a step-by-step approach. Rushing through diagnostics without understanding the problem can lead to further complications.

Warning: Always back up your data before making changes to boot configurations or using repair tools like `fsck`. Incorrect usage may result in data loss.

The Role of Boot Troubleshooting

- **Ensures System Accessibility:** Boot troubleshooting ensures that the system starts properly and is accessible to users.
- **Key Tasks:**
    - Diagnosing and fixing issues related to BIOS/UEFI, GRUB, kernel, and system initialization.
    - Preventing downtime and restoring functionality for smooth operations.

Best Practices for Boot Troubleshooting:
- Maintain a bootable Live CD or USB for emergencies.
- Regularly update and test GRUB configurations after kernel updates.
- Document any changes made to bootloader settings for future reference.

Key Characteristics of Boot Troubleshooting

- **Critical for System Accessibility:** Boot issues can prevent the system from becoming operational.
- **Requires Step-by-Step Diagnostics:** The multi-stage boot process requires careful attention at each phase.
- **Tools for Precise Diagnosis:** Tools like grub-mkconfig, Live CDs, and boot logs are indispensable for resolving issues.
- **Recovery Mode and Logs:** Recovery mode and /var/log/boot.log are vital resources for identifying errors.
- **Time-Sensitive:** Rapid fixes are essential to minimize downtime and disruptions.

Understanding the Linux Boot Process

- **Stages of the Boot Process:**
    1. **BIOS/UEFI Initialization:** Hardware initialization, hardware checks, and boot device selection.
    2. **Bootloader:** Loads and transfers control to the kernel.
    3. **Kernel Initialization:** Handles hardware detection and mounts the root filesystem.
    4. **System Startup:** Executes system initialization and user services.
- **Explanation:** Each stage plays a critical role in ensuring a successful boot.

BIOS/UEFI Initialization

- **Role of BIOS/UEFI:** Basic hardware initialization, including hardware checks and boot device selection.
- **Differences between BIOS and UEFI:** UEFI is more advanced, supporting faster booting and larger drives.
- **Common Issue:** No display or black screen due to incorrect BIOS/UEFI settings.
    - **Solution:** Check boot device order and reset to default settings if necessary.

Warning: Incorrect BIOS/UEFI updates can render your system unbootable. Always follow manufacturer guidelines.

Bootloader Stages and Kernel Initialization

- **Bootloader Overview:** Essential for starting Linux by locating and loading the kernel.
- **Stages of Bootloader:** Loading the kernel and passing control to it.
- **Kernel Initialization:** Detects hardware and initializes system components.
- **Common Issue:** Boot stops after BIOS/UEFI due to bootloader or kernel issues.
  - **Solution:** Reinstall or configure the bootloader (e.g., GRUB).

Common Boot Problems

1. **GRUB Errors:** Often caused by misconfigurations or missing files.
   - **Solution:** Regenerate GRUB configuration using grub-mkconfig.
2. **Missing Kernel:** Kernel not found or loaded.
   - **Solution:** Use a Live CD to restore or reinstall the kernel.
3. **Init Failures:** Problems initializing system services.
   - **Solution:** Inspect /etc/fstab or init scripts.
4. **Issues with initramfs:** Missing or corrupted initramfs.
   - **Solution:** Rebuild initramfs using mkinitcpio or similar tools.

Tools for Diagnosing Boot Issues

Tool	Purpose	Example Command
Boot Recovery Mode	Access for troubleshooting	Select from GRUB menu
Analyzing Boot Logs	Identify issues in boot process	`cat /var/log/boot.log`
Live CD	Repair bootloaders and configurations	Use tools like `chroot` and `grub-install`

Best Practice: Keep a detailed record of boot configurations and errors to expedite future troubleshooting.

Real-Life Troubleshooting Example

Scenario: GRUB Error After Update

A user updates their Linux system and notices that the system no longer boots, displaying a "GRUB rescue>" prompt. Here's how the issue is diagnosed and resolved:

1. **Identify the Problem:**
   o *The GRUB configuration* is missing or corrupted after the update.
2. **Access Recovery Mode:**
   o Boot using a Live CD or recovery USB.

Mount the root partition of the affected system:

```
sudo mount /dev/sda1 /mnt
```

3. **Prepare the Environment:**

Mount necessary filesystems to replicate the system environment:

```
sudo mount --bind /dev /mnt/dev
sudo mount --bind /proc /mnt/proc
sudo mount --bind /sys /mnt/sys
```

4. Chroot into the System:

Change the root to the mounted system:

```
sudo chroot /mnt
```

5. Repair GRUB:

Reinstall GRUB:

```
grub-install /dev/sda
```

Regenerate the GRUB configuration:

```
grub-mkconfig -o /boot/grub/grub.cfg
```

6. Exit and Reboot:

Exit the chroot environment:

```
exit
```

Unmount the filesystems and reboot the system:

```
sudo umount /mnt/{dev,proc,sys}
sudo umount /mnt
sudo reboot
```

7. Verify:

- Confirm that the GRUB menu appears and the system boots correctly.

Practice Section (Hands-on with Boot Issues)

1. **Exercises:**
   - Diagnose and fix boot issues using
   ```
   /var/log/boot.log.
   ```
   - Access recovery mode to troubleshoot missing kernel issues.
   - Regenerate GRUB configuration using grub-mkconfig.
2. **Boot Issue Challenge:** Use a combination of tools to troubleshoot and resolve boot failures.

Summary and Glossary

- **Key Takeaways:**
  - Understanding the Linux boot process helps diagnose and resolve issues effectively.
  - Tools like GRUB recovery mode, boot logs, and Live CDs are essential for troubleshooting.
- **Glossary:**
  - **BIOS/UEFI:** Firmware initializing hardware and managing the boot process.
  - **GRUB:** Bootloader managing the startup of Linux and other operating systems.
  - **initramfs:** Initial RAM file system used during the boot process.

Chapter 5: Managing File System Issues

Understanding Linux file systems is critical for efficient system management. This chapter explores diagnosing and resolving file system issues, managing disk space, and using tools to maintain system integrity.

Key Focus Areas

- **Troubleshooting file system errors:** Identify and resolve common issues.
- **Optimizing disk usage:** Learn tools and techniques to keep your system running efficiently.
- **Recovery tools:** Understand and use utilities to recover lost data and repair damaged file systems.

Note: Proactively monitoring and managing file systems minimizes downtime and prevents severe issues.

The Role of File System Management

Importance

1. **Storage Organization:** File systems ensure efficient data retrieval and storage.
2. **System Performance:** Regular monitoring prevents slowdowns and crashes.
3. **Data Protection:** Tools like fsck maintain data integrity after unexpected shutdowns.

Warning: Running fsck or other tools on mounted file systems can lead to data corruption. Always unmount before performing repairs.

Key Characteristics of File System Management

Characteristic	Benefit
Directory Hierarchy	Simplifies file organization and access
Efficiency	Prevents slowdowns and resource wastage
Automation	Reduces manual intervention
Recovery Tools	Enables quick restoration of lost data

Best Practice: Automate regular cleanups and backups to ensure file system health and system reliability.

Understanding File System Layouts and Mount Points

Concepts

- **File System:** A method for organizing and accessing data.
- **Mount Points:** Directories where file systems are made accessible.
- **File System Types:** Common types include ext4, Btrfs, and XFS.
  Simplified Example: Mounting an external drive:

```
sudo mount /dev/sdb1 /mnt/backup
```

Note: Verify mount points after updates or disk changes to avoid accidental overwriting.

Key Directories and Their Functions

Directory	Function	Example Issue
/etc	Stores system configuration files	Corrupted file preventing boot
/var	Contains logs and growing data	Full /var causing service interruptions
/tmp	Temporary files created by processes	Excessive files slowing down the system

Warning: Avoid manually deleting files in critical directories like /etc without thorough understanding.

Diagnosing Disk and File System Errors

Common Issues

1. **Disk Space Shortages:** Applications fail due to insufficient space.
2. **File System Corruption:** Caused by improper shutdowns or hardware issues.

Tools and Commands

Tool	Purpose	Example Command
df	Displays disk space usage	df -h
du	Analyzes directory sizes	du -sh /var
fsck	Checks and repairs file systems	sudo fsck /dev/sda1

Real-Life Troubleshooting Example

Scenario: Application Failure Due to Disk Full

1. **Identify the Problem:**
   - Check disk usage with df -h.
   - Result: /var partition is full.
2. **Find Large Files:**
   - Use du -sh /var/* to locate large directories.
   - Result: Logs in /var/log are consuming excessive space.
3. **Resolve the Issue:**

Remove old logs:

```
sudo find /var/log -type f -mtime +30 -delete
```

4. **Verify Free Space:**
   - Recheck with df -h.

Best Practice: Automate log rotation using tools like logrotate to prevent recurring issues.

Using fsck for File System Checks

Simplified Process

Unmount the file system:

```
sudo umount /dev/sda1
```

Run fsck:

```
sudo fsck /dev/sda1
```

Remount the file system:

```
sudo mount /dev/sda1 /mnt
```

Warning: Never interrupt fsck while it's running, as this may worsen corruption.

Best Practices for File System Management

Recommendations

1. **Monitor Regularly:**
   - Use tools like df and du for disk health.
   - Set alerts for critical disk usage thresholds.
2. **Automate Cleanup:**
   - Schedule periodic file deletions using cron jobs.
   - Rotate logs to save space in directories like /var/log.

3. **Back Up Frequently:**
   - Implement daily or weekly backups.
   - Use tools like rsync for incremental backups.

Note: Always test backup and recovery plans to ensure they function correctly.

Automating Disk Space Management

Example Script

Automate log cleanup to free up space:

```bash
#!/bin/bash
find /var/log -type f -mtime +30 -exec rm -f {} \;
```

Real-Life Application: Schedule this script to run weekly to prevent disk shortages.

Summary and Glossary

Key Takeaways

- Effective file system management ensures data safety and system stability.
- Tools like fsck, du, and df are essential for troubleshooting.

Glossary

Term	Definition
df	Command to check disk space usage
du	Command to analyze directory sizes
fsck	Utility for repairing file systems
File System Types	Formats like ext4, Btrfs, and XFS for organizing data

Chapter 6: Troubleshooting Memory and CPU Issues

Diagnosing and troubleshooting memory and CPU problems is essential for Linux system administrators to ensure optimal system performance. This chapter provides detailed guidance on identifying and resolving issues like memory leaks, high CPU usage, and system slowdowns, using practical tools and techniques.

Key Focus Areas

- **Memory management:** Detect and address memory leaks and high memory usage.
- **CPU troubleshooting:** Identify and mitigate high CPU utilization and bottlenecks.
- **Tools and techniques:** Learn essential commands and utilities for diagnosing memory and CPU-related problems.

    Real-Life Application: Effective troubleshooting improves system performance, prevents crashes, and optimizes resources for smoother operations.

The Role of Memory and CPU in System Performance

Core Functions

1. **Memory (RAM):** Temporary storage for quick access to data by the CPU. Memory holds active programs and processes to ensure fast performance.
2. **CPU (Central Processing Unit):** Executes instructions, processes tasks, and drives the operations of software.
3. **Resource Management:** Efficient utilization ensures systems remain responsive and handle workloads effectively.
   Best Practice: Regularly monitor resource usage using diagnostic tools to detect anomalies before they impact performance.

Real-Life Context

- A high-traffic web server requires balanced CPU and memory allocation to handle requests efficiently.
- Insufficient memory can lead to excessive swapping, degrading performance.
- Overloaded CPUs can cause delayed task execution or complete system freezes.

Key Characteristics of Memory and CPU Management

Characteristic	Benefit
Memory Usage	Efficient use of RAM prevents slowdowns
CPU Load	Balanced CPU utilization avoids bottlenecks
Resource Bottlenecks	Early detection prevents cascading issues
System Responsiveness	Ensures stable and fast system performance

Note: High resource usage isn't inherently bad but should align with the workload demands of the system.

Diagnosing Memory Problems

Signs of Memory Issues

- **Slow system response:** Delays in opening applications or processing tasks.
- **Application crashes:** Programs terminate unexpectedly due to insufficient memory.
- **High swap usage:** Indicates RAM exhaustion, causing data to move to slower disk storage.

Tools for Diagnosis

Tool	Purpose	Example Command
free	Displays memory usage statistics	free -h
vmstat	Monitors memory, processes, and I/O	vmstat 1
smem	Provides detailed memory usage by process	smem -r

Real-Life Example: A web server with delayed response times can use free to check if memory is fully utilized and smem to identify which processes consume the most memory.

Using `free`, `vmstat`, and `smem` to Monitor Memory

Simplified Commands

Check total and free memory:

```
free -h
```

Displays the total, used, and free memory in a human-readable format.
Monitor memory and process stats:

```
vmstat 1
```

Outputs real-time statistics for memory, processes, and I/O activity every second.
Analyze memory usage by process:

```
smem -r
```

Displays detailed memory breakdowns, including shared memory and resident memory used by each process.

> **Warning:** Consistently high memory usage can result in slower system performance and trigger the OOM Killer.

Analyzing Memory Leaks

What is a Memory Leak?

A memory leak occurs when an application allocates memory but fails to release it after use, causing it to consume more RAM over time.

Signs of Memory Leaks

- Gradual increase in memory usage over time.
- Applications becoming unresponsive or crashing frequently.

Detection Tools

Tool	Purpose	Example Command
valgrind	Detects memory leaks in applications	valgrind ./app
top	Monitors memory usage by processes	top -o %MEM

Real-Life Example: A database application gradually consumes all available memory due to a memory leak. Use top to identify the process and valgrind to locate the issue in the application code.

Understanding the OOM Killer

The Out of Memory (OOM) Killer is a Linux feature that terminates processes to free up memory when the system runs out of RAM.

Common Triggers

- Insufficient available memory.
- Excessive memory usage by a single process.

Mitigation Strategies

1. **Adjust process memory limits:** Use ulimit to set caps on memory usage.

2. **Increase swap space:** Allocate more swap to handle memory overflow.
3. **Monitor memory usage:** Regular checks prevent excessive consumption.

   Real-Life Example: When a system crashes due to memory exhaustion, review logs in /var/log/syslog or dmesg to identify processes terminated by the OOM Killer.

Troubleshooting High CPU Usage

Symptoms

- Sluggish system performance.
- Excessive fan noise indicating thermal stress.
- Applications freezing or failing to respond.

Diagnostic Tools

Tool	Purpose	Example Command
top	Displays CPU usage by process in real-time	top -o %CPU
pidstat	Provides detailed CPU usage statistics	pidstat -u 1

   Real-Life Example: A runaway script causes a CPU spike. Use top to locate the process and either kill it or lower its priority.

Managing Resource-Intensive Tasks

Tools for Management

nice: Sets the priority of a process when it starts.

```
nice -n 10 process_name
```

renice: Adjusts the priority of an already running process.

```
renice -n 10 -p PID
```

> **Real-Life Example:** Lower the priority of a backup job using nice to ensure it doesn't interfere with critical tasks.

Tuning Performance for Resource Bottlenecks

Identifying Bottlenecks

Use tools like vmstat, top, and iotop to detect the resource being maxed out.

Optimization Techniques

Resource	Optimization Strategy
Memory	Add RAM or optimize swap usage
CPU	Distribute workloads across multiple cores

Real-Life Example: When CPU usage spikes during large data processing tasks, adjust task priorities or utilize multi-threading to distribute the load.

Configuring CPU Affinity for Better Load Balancing

CPU affinity binds specific processes to particular CPU cores, optimizing performance for multi-core systems.

Example Command

Bind a process to CPU cores 0 and 1:

```
taskset -c 0,1 process_name
```

Best Practice: Assign resource-intensive processes to specific cores to minimize their impact on other system tasks.

Summary and Glossary

- Monitor and diagnose memory and CPU issues using tools like free, smem, and top.
- Optimize resource usage through task prioritization and system tuning.

Glossary

Term	Definition
nice	Sets process priority during startup
renice	Adjusts priority of running processes
taskset	Binds processes to specific CPU cores
OOM Killer	Linux mechanism for handling out-of-memory scenarios

Chapter 7: Network Troubleshooting

Learn how to diagnose and fix network-related issues in Linux systems, including checking connections, resolving DNS problems, identifying firewall issues, and analyzing packets for deeper insights.

Network troubleshooting is essential for maintaining communication between devices, ensuring internet connectivity, and optimizing server functionality. This chapter provides tools and techniques to identify and resolve network problems.

> **Real-Life Application:** Network issues can disrupt internet access, prevent communication with servers, and cause downtime. By mastering network troubleshooting, administrators can restore functionality and optimize system performance.

The Role of Networking in System Administration

Core Functions

1. **Networking in Linux:** Facilitates communication between systems, access to the internet, and management of servers.
2. **Network Configuration:** Proper setup of interfaces, IP addresses, and routing tables ensures seamless communication.
3. **Problem-Solving:** Diagnosing and resolving network issues improves system performance and restores connectivity.

> **Best Practice:** Regularly verify network configurations and test connectivity to prevent unexpected outages.

Key Characteristics of Network Troubleshooting

Characteristic	Importance
Connectivity	Ensures systems communicate effectively
Configuration	Proper setup prevents miscommunication
Security	Identifying and resolving firewall issues
Advanced Analysis	Enables deeper investigation into issues

Note: Network troubleshooting often requires both basic tools (like ping) and advanced analysis tools (like tcpdump).

Understanding Network Configuration

Key Components

1. **Network Interfaces:** Represent devices used to connect to networks (e.g., eth0, wlan0).
2. **IP Addresses:** Unique identifiers for devices on a network.
3. **Routing Tables:** Direct traffic to appropriate destinations.

Simplified Example

If a system cannot access the internet:
- **Check Interface:** Verify the status of the interface with ip link.
- **Verify IP Configuration:** Confirm IP settings with ip addr.
- **Inspect Routing Table:** Use ip route to check routing paths.
  Real-Life Example: A server's inability to access the internet might stem from a missing gateway in the routing table.

Diagnosing Connectivity Issues

Symptoms

- Inability to reach devices, websites, or servers.
- Slow internet speeds or frequent connection drops.

Diagnostic Tools

Tool	Purpose	Example Command
`ping`	Checks connectivity to a target	`ping google.com`
`traceroute`	Displays the route data takes to a destination	`traceroute google.com`
`mtr`	Combines ping and traceroute for live stats	`mtr google.com`

Real-Life Example: Use `ping` to verify if a server is reachable. If not, `traceroute` can reveal where the connection is failing.

Checking Link Status with `ethtool`

A utility for inspecting and configuring Ethernet device settings.

Key Functions

- **Check Link Status:** Verify if the link is active, and review speed and duplex settings.

Example Command:

```
ethtool eth0
```

> **Real-Life Example:** Troubleshoot a slow Ethernet connection by using ethtool to confirm if the link speed matches expected values (e.g., 1 Gbps).

Troubleshooting Wireless Networking Issues

Common Problems

- Weak or unstable Wi-Fi signals.
- Authentication failures.
- Misconfigured wireless interfaces.

Tools and Commands

Tool	Purpose	Example Command
iwconfig	Configures and checks wireless settings	iwconfig wlan0
nmcli	Manages network connections	nmcli dev wifi connect SSID
iw	Advanced wireless management	iw dev wlan0 link

> **Real-Life Example:** A laptop cannot connect to Wi-Fi. Use nmcli to verify available networks and reconfigure the connection.

Network Performance Testing

Purpose

Measure network throughput, latency, and bandwidth to identify performance bottlenecks.

Tools and Commands

Tool	Purpose	Example Command
iperf	Tests bandwidth between two systems	iperf3 —s (server), iperf3 —c <server>
speedtest—cli	Measures internet speed	speedtest—cli

Real-Life Example: If file transfers are slow, use iperf to test bandwidth between the systems and identify if the issue is network-related.

Network Interface Troubleshooting

Common Issues

- Interface down or disconnected.
- Incorrect IP configuration.

Tools and Commands

Tool	Purpose	Example Command
ip link	Shows interface status	ip link show
ifconfig	**Checks** interface configuration	ifconfig eth0
dhclient	Requests an IP address from DHCP	sudo dhclient eth0

Real-Life Example: If an Ethernet connection is not working, use ip link to ensure the interface is up and dhclient to renew the IP address.

Basic Network File Transfer Troubleshooting

Tools

Tool	Purpose	Example Command
scp	Securely copies files between systems	scp file user@remote:/path
rsync	Synchronizes files over the network	rsync -av file remote:/path

Real-Life Example: When file transfers fail, verify SSH connectivity for scp or ensure correct path configuration for rsync.

Resolving Firewall and Port Issues

Firewall Tools

Tool	Purpose	Example Command
iptables	Configures packet filtering rules	iptables -L
ufw	Simplifies firewall management	ufw status
nmap	Scans for open ports and services	nmap localhost

Real-Life Example

If SSH access is blocked:

1. Use nmap to verify if port 22 is open.
2. Check iptables rules or ufw status to ensure SSH is allowed.

Advanced Network Debugging

Capturing Packets with tcpdump

Basic Command:

```
tcpdump -i eth0
```
   o   Captures all packets on eth0.

Filtered Capture:

```
tcpdump -i eth0 port 80
```

○ Captures only HTTP traffic.

Real-Life Example: Analyze intermittent network issues by capturing and reviewing packets to identify anomalies or dropped connections.

Common Troubleshooting Pitfalls

Checklist

1. Overlooking physical connections.
2. Neglecting to restart network services after configuration changes.
3. Ignoring DNS cache issues.
4. Skipping firewall checks during troubleshooting.
5. Using outdated network drivers.

Best Practice: Follow a structured approach to troubleshoot issues systematically.

Real-Life Troubleshooting Example

Scenario: Website Access Failure

1. **Verify Connectivity:**
   ○ Use ping google.com to check if the domain is reachable.
2. **Check DNS Resolution:**
   ○ Use nslookup to verify DNS resolves correctly.
3. **Inspect Firewall:**
   ○ Use ufw status or iptables −L to check for blocked ports.
4. **Capture Traffic:**
   ○ Use tcpdump to analyze HTTP traffic on port 80.

Outcome: Identified a DNS misconfiguration in /etc/resolv. conf, corrected it, and restored website access.

Summary and Glossary

- Use basic tools like ping and traceroute for connectivity checks.
- Resolve DNS issues by verifying configurations and clearing caches.
- Manage firewalls effectively to ensure access while maintaining security.
- Capture and analyze network traffic with tcpdump for advanced troubleshooting.

Glossary

Term	Definition
ping	Tests connectivity to a target IP
traceroute	Displays the path packets take to a destination
ethtool	Inspects and configures Ethernet devices
iptables	Manages packet filtering rules
nmap	Scans for open ports and services
tcpdump	Captures and analyzes network traffic

Chapter 8: Application and Service Troubleshooting

Learn how to troubleshoot issues with applications and services on a Linux system, identify common errors, and apply solutions.

Application and service issues are common in Linux systems. Diagnosing and resolving these issues often requires understanding how services interact with system resources and dependencies. This chapter provides detailed instructions and real-world examples to equip you with the tools and knowledge needed for efficient troubleshooting.

> **Real-Life Application:** If a service fails to start or an application behaves unexpectedly, you need to investigate the root cause. This chapter will help you use system tools to identify and fix problems efficiently.

The Role of Services and Applications in System Administration

Core Functions

1. **Services:** Background processes (daemons) that provide essential functionality (e.g., web servers, database services).
2. **Applications:** Software used by users, such as text editors, browsers, or productivity tools.
3. **Problem-Solving:** Service failures or application crashes can disrupt normal system operation. Efficient troubleshooting is critical to minimize downtime and maintain system stability.

> **Best Practice:** Regularly monitor services and applications using tools like `systemctl` and logs to detect issues early.

Key Characteristics of Application and Service Troubleshooting

Characteristic	Importance
Service Management	Ensures critical services run without errors
Dependency Management	Resolves issues preventing proper functionality
Resource Conflicts	Identifies and resolves resource conflicts
Logging and Debugging	Provides insights into failures via logs
Package Management	Repairs or reinstalls application packages

Note: Understanding how services interact with system resources is crucial for effective troubleshooting.

Diagnosing Service Failures

Symptoms

- Service not starting.
- Service hanging or crashing unexpectedly.

Tools for Diagnosis

Tool	Purpose	Example Command
systemctl	Controls services	systemctl status apache2
journalctl	Displays logs for systemd services	journalctl -u apache2
Service Logs	Identifies the cause of service failure	tail -f /var/log/syslog

Detailed Steps

1. **Check Service Status:** Use systemctl to view whether the service is active or inactive.
2. **Examine Logs:** Open the relevant service logs with journalctl or tail to identify specific errors or warnings.
3. **Test Restart:** Attempt to restart the service with systemctl restart. Note any error messages that appear.

   Real-Life Example: If Apache fails to start, systemctl might indicate a configuration error. Use journalctl -u apache2 to find a specific line pointing to the problematic configuration.

Checking Dependencies and Configurations

Common Issues

1. **Dependency Issues:** Services often rely on other services or libraries.
2. **Configuration Errors:** Incorrect settings in configuration files can prevent services from starting.

Tools and Commands

Tool	Purpose	Example Command
`systemctl show`	Displays service dependencies	`systemctl show apache2`
Configuration Files	Stores settings for services	`/etc/httpd/httpd.conf`

Steps to Diagnose

1. **Verify Dependencies:** Use `systemctl show` to list all dependencies for the failing service.
2. **Inspect Configuration Files:** Open the configuration file in a text editor, such as nano or vim. Check for syntax errors or missing directives.

Test Configuration: Some services, like Apache, allow you to test configurations directly:
apachectl configtest

> **Real-Life Example:** If Apache's httpd.conf file contains an invalid directive, the test will fail. Correct the error and restart the service.

Common Application Issues

Symptoms

- Application fails to open.
- Frequent crashes or unexpected behavior.

Troubleshooting Steps

1. **Check Logs:** Application logs often reveal the root cause of failures. Look for log files in /var/log/ or within the application directory.
2. **Trace System Calls:** Use strace to identify where the application fails.
3. **Review Configurations:** Ensure configuration files are correct and complete.
4. **Check for Missing Libraries:** Use ldd to verify that all required libraries are installed.

Example

Command:

```
strace -e trace=open myapp
```

   o   Traces file access errors, revealing missing or inaccessible files.
- **Log Inspection:** Open the log file, e.g., /var/log/myapp.log, to find error details.

   Real-Life Example: If a text editor fails to start, it might be due to missing libraries or misconfiguration. Use strace to track system calls and identify the problem.

Resolving Port Conflicts

Port conflicts occur when multiple services try to use the same port (e.g., two web servers on port 80).

Tools for Diagnosis

Tool	Purpose	Example Command
ss	Shows socket statistics and port usage	ss -tuln
lsof	Lists open files and ports	lsof -i :80

Steps

1. **Identify Conflicts:** Use ss or lsof to determine which process is using the conflicting port.
2. **Resolve Conflicts:** Stop the conflicting process or configure one of the services to use a different port.
3. **Restart Service:** Restart the service after resolving the conflict.
   Real-Life Example: If a web server cannot start, use ss to find which service is using port 80, then reconfigure or stop the conflicting process.

Debugging with strace and lsof

Tool	Purpose	Example Command
strace	Traces system calls made by applications	strace -e trace=open myapp
lsof	Lists files and network connections	lsof -p 1234

Detailed Steps

1. **Trace System Calls:** Use strace to identify where a program fails by monitoring its system calls.
2. **Check Open Files:** Use lsof to view files being accessed by a process.

   Real-Life Example: If an application crashes when accessing a file, use strace to trace system calls and lsof to identify file access issues.

Crash Handling and Core Dumps

Steps to Enable Core Dumps

Enable Core Dumps:

```
ulimit -c unlimited
```

Analyze with gdb:

```
gdb /path/to/application core
```

Detailed Example

Enable Core Dumps for Service:

```
echo '/tmp/core.%e.%p' > /proc/sys/kernel/core_pattern
```

1. **Simulate and Capture Crash:** Run the application to trigger a crash and generate a core file.
2. **Debug:** Use gdb to load the core dump and investigate the issue.

   Real-Life Example: Debug an application crash by analyzing the core dump using gdb to identify the source of the error.

Configuration Management Tips

Best Practices

1. **Version Control:** Use `git` to track changes in configuration files.
2. **Backups:** Regularly back up critical configuration files.
3. **Automation:** Use tools like `Ansible` or `Puppet` to manage configurations across multiple systems.

   Real-Life Example: Maintain a Git repository for `/etc/` to quickly identify and revert problematic changes.

Common Troubleshooting Pitfalls

Checklist

1. Skipping log analysis.
2. Overlooking dependency issues.
3. Failing to restart services after configuration changes.
4. Ignoring resource conflicts.
5. Not testing changes in a safe environment.
   Best Practice: Always follow a structured troubleshooting approach and test changes in a controlled environment.

Real-Life Troubleshooting Example

Scenario: Nginx Service Fails to Start

Check Service Status:

```
systemctl status nginx
```

View Logs:

```
journalctl -u nginx
```

Analyze Configuration:

```
nginx -t
```

o Fix any syntax errors in the configuration file.

Resolve Port Conflicts:

```
ss -tuln | grep 80
```

o Stop the conflicting service or change the port in the configuration.

Outcome: After resolving the issues, the Nginx service starts successfully.

Summary and Glossary

- Use tools like systemctl, journalctl, and lsof to diagnose and resolve application and service issues.
- Manage dependencies with ldd and package managers.

Glossary

Term	Definition
systemctl	Manages system services
journalctl	Displays logs for systemd services
strace	Traces system calls for debugging
lsof	Lists open files and network connections
ldd	Lists shared library dependencies
gdb	Debugging tool for analyzing core dumps

Chapter 9: Kernel Troubleshooting

Learn how to troubleshoot kernel-related issues in Linux systems, including handling kernel panics, reading kernel logs, and managing kernel modules.

Kernel issues are critical as they affect the core functionality of your system. This chapter will help you understand how to diagnose and resolve problems related to the Linux kernel, using tools and techniques for reading kernel logs, managing drivers and modules, and handling kernel panics.

> **Real-Life Application:** If your system crashes or behaves unpredictably, it could be due to kernel-level issues. Diagnosing these problems requires understanding the kernel's role and using the right tools to resolve conflicts.

The Role of the Kernel in System Administration

Core Functions

1. **The Kernel's Role:** The kernel is the core component of the operating system that manages hardware resources and system processes. It acts as an intermediary between hardware and software.
2. **Why Kernel Troubleshooting Matters:** Kernel issues can cause system crashes, freezes, and instability, impacting both user applications and system services. Efficient kernel troubleshooting is crucial to maintaining a stable Linux environment.
3. **Problem-Solving:** Troubleshooting kernel issues requires interpreting error messages, analyzing logs, and resolving driver or module conflicts.

Best Practice: Keep your kernel updated to ensure compatibility and security.

Key Characteristics of Kernel Troubleshooting

Characteristic	Importance
Kernel Logs	Identifies hardware and software errors.
Kernel Panics	Diagnoses and resolves critical system crashes.
Driver and Module Management	Ensures compatibility and functionality of hardware.
Tools and Commands	Provides essential utilities for diagnostics.

Note: Proactive monitoring of kernel logs can prevent many potential issues.

Understanding Kernel Logs and Errors

Kernel logs contain messages related to hardware, drivers, modules, and system events at the kernel level. These logs help identify issues such as hardware failures, module conflicts, or crashes.

Where to Find Kernel Logs

1. **dmesg Command:** Displays messages from the kernel buffer, including boot-time messages, hardware information, and error messages.
2. **Log Files:** Kernel logs are often stored in /var/log/kern.log (if configured).
3. **journalctl:** On systems using systemd, view kernel logs with journalctl -k.

Reading dmesg Output

Command	Purpose
dmesg	Displays all kernel messages.
`dmesg	grep error`

Real-Life Example: Use dmesg to check for hardware initialization errors after boot.

Logging Kernel Warnings and Panics

A kernel panic is a system error that occurs when the kernel encounters a critical issue it cannot recover from, often resulting in the system freezing or crashing.

Handling Kernel Panics

1. **Symptoms:** The system may freeze, display a message like "Kernel Panic," or reboot unexpectedly.
2. **Diagnosing Kernel Panics:** Use kernel logs (dmesg, /var/log/kern. log, journalctl −k) to identify the cause of the panic, such as hardware failure or faulty drivers.
3. **Recovering from a Panic:** Boot into recovery mode or use a Live CD to troubleshoot and repair the issue.
   Real-Life Example: A kernel panic due to bad RAM will display errors in the kernel logs indicating memory faults. Use memtest86 to diagnose and replace the faulty RAM.

Handling Kernel Panics

Common Causes

Cause	Description
Faulty Hardware	Bad RAM, hard disks, or peripherals causing crashes.
Driver Issues	Incompatible or corrupt drivers causing instability.
Corrupted File Systems	Root file system corruption leading to boot failure.

Steps to Handle a Kernel Panic

1. **Check Logs:** Use dmesg or journalctl to identify errors leading up to the panic.
2. **Test Hardware:** Use diagnostic tools to check memory (memtest86) and storage health (smartctl).
3. **Update or Reinstall Drivers:** Update the affected driver or module causing the panic.
4. **Boot in Recovery Mode:** Use a recovery kernel or Live CD to troubleshoot.

   Best Practice: Keep backups of critical files and regularly test hardware to prevent unexpected failures.

Interpreting Panic Messages and Stack Traces

Kernel panic messages include error codes, descriptions, and stack traces. These provide a detailed report of the kernel's state at the time of the panic.

How to Read Stack Traces

Component	Purpose
Error Codes	Indicate hardware or software failures.
Function Calls	List kernel functions active during the crash.

Example

A panic message indicating ata1: hard reset failed points to an issue with the hard drive or its driver. Use logs and diagnostic tools to investigate further.

> **Tools:** Use dmesg, journalctl, and online kernel documentation to decode error messages.

Resolving Driver and Module Issues

What are Kernel Modules?

Kernel modules are pieces of code that extend the kernel's functionality, managing hardware devices like network cards, graphics cards, and storage controllers.

Common Module Issues

1. **Incompatibility:** Modules not compatible with the kernel version.
2. **Missing Dependencies:** Modules require other modules or files to function.

Managing Modules

Command	Purpose
modprobe	Loads or unloads kernel modules.
lsmod	Lists all currently loaded modules.

Real-Life Example: If a Wi-Fi card isn't working, load the iwlwifi module using modprobe.

Kernel Updates and Maintenance

Importance of Kernel Updates

- Regular updates ensure security patches, compatibility, and bug fixes.
- Prevent issues caused by outdated drivers or kernel versions.

Commands for Kernel Updates

Command	Purpose
apt-get install	Installs new kernel versions in Debian-based systems.
yum update kernel	Updates the kernel in Red Hat-based systems.

Real-Life Example: Update the kernel to resolve hardware compatibility issues or apply critical security fixes.

Advanced Diagnostic Tools

Tools for Kernel Diagnostics

Tool	Purpose
kdump	Captures kernel crash dumps for analysis.
crash	Analyzes kernel crash dumps.

Best Practice: Configure kdump to capture dumps for post-mortem analysis.

Proactive Monitoring

Tools and Techniques

sysctl: Adjust kernel parameters for performance or debugging.

```
sysctl -w kernel.panic=10
```

1. **kexec:** Allows faster kernel reboots for testing or updates.

   Real-Life Example: Use sysctl to modify kernel panic behavior for automated reboots.

Filesystem-Specific Troubleshooting

Handling Filesystem Issues

1. Use fsck to check and repair filesystem errors.
2. Monitor specific logs for filesystem-related issues (e.g., /var/log/syslog).

   Real-Life Example: If a kernel panic occurs during boot due to a corrupted filesystem, use a recovery kernel and fsck to resolve the issue.

Virtualization and Kernel Issues

Common Issues in Virtualized Environments

1. Kernel module conflicts in virtual machines.
2. Performance degradation due to misconfigured kernel parameters.

Solutions

- Optimize kernel parameters for virtualized workloads.
- Use virtualization-aware kernel modules.

   Real-Life Example: Troubleshoot a slow VMware guest OS by adjusting kernel I/O scheduler parameters.

Security Considerations

Kernel Hardening Techniques

1. Enable SELinux or AppArmor for enhanced security.
2. Apply patches for known vulnerabilities.

Best Practice: Regularly scan for vulnerabilities and apply kernel patches.

Kernel Configuration and Compilation

Steps for Custom Kernel Compilation

1. Download kernel source code.
2. Configure options with make menuconfig.
3. Compile and install the kernel.

    Real-Life Example: Compile a custom kernel to enable specific hardware support or debugging features.

Common Pitfalls in Kernel Troubleshooting

Checklist

1. Neglecting to back up before updates.
2. Forgetting to match module versions with the kernel.
3. Overlooking logs during panic analysis.
4. Using incorrect kernel parameters.

    Best Practice: Always test changes in a controlled environment before applying them to production systems.

Real-Life Troubleshooting Example
Scenario: Kernel Panic on Boot

1. **Symptoms:** System fails to boot, displaying a kernel panic message.
2. **Steps:**
    - Boot into recovery mode.
    - Use dmesg and journalctl to identify the error.
    - Load missing modules with modprobe.
    - Repair the filesystem with fsck if needed.
3. **Outcome:** Resolving these issues allows the system to boot normally, preventing further downtime.

Summary and Glossary

Key Takeaways

- Kernel logs are essential for identifying and resolving issues.
- Kernel panics require careful diagnosis and recovery steps.

Glossary

Term	Definition
Kernel Panic	A critical error causing the system to crash.
modprobe	Command for loading and unloading kernel modules.
dmesg	Displays messages from the kernel buffer.
lsmod	Lists all currently loaded kernel modules.
Stack Trace	Detailed report of kernel function calls.

Chapter 10: User and Permission Issues

This chapter will cover how to troubleshoot common user and permission-related issues in Linux systems. You will learn to diagnose login problems, understand and fix permission errors, and resolve account lockouts.

In a multi-user system, managing user accounts and permissions is critical for security and functionality. Problems related to user access, permissions, and authentication can prevent users from logging in, accessing files, or performing certain tasks. This chapter will help you understand how to fix these issues using various Linux tools.

> **Real-Life Application:** If a user can't log in or access certain files, this chapter will guide you through diagnosing and solving those issues efficiently.

The Role of User and Permission Management in System Administration

Core Functions

1. **Managing User Accounts and Permissions:** Administering user access and controlling who can read, write, and execute files is fundamental to Linux system administration.
2. **Why It Matters:** Incorrect permissions or login issues can lock users out of important files and systems, affecting productivity and security.
3. **Problem-Solving:** Troubleshooting user issues involves diagnosing account-related problems, understanding permissions, and managing authentication methods.

Best Practice: Regularly review user accounts and permissions to maintain security and functionality.

Key Characteristics of Troubleshooting User and Permission Issues

Characteristic	Importance
Authentication	Resolves login issues caused by password or SSH problems.
Permissions	Ensures proper file access and prevents unauthorized changes.
Account Lockouts	Resolves issues from failed login attempts or expired passwords.
Tools and Commands	Provides essential utilities like passwd, chmod, and faillog for diagnostics.

Note: User and permission management is essential for system security and user productivity.

Real-Life Troubleshooting Example

Scenario: Locked-Out Root User

1. **Issue:** The root account is locked after multiple incorrect login attempts.
2. **Steps to Resolve:**
   - Boot into recovery mode.

Mount the filesystem as writable:

```
mount -o remount,rw /
```

Use passwd to reset the root password:

```
passwd root
```

Unlock the account:

```
passwd -u root
```

3. **Outcome:** The root account is restored, and the administrator can log in.

    Real-Life Impact: Prevents prolonged downtime by restoring administrative access to the system.

Best Practices for User and Permission Management

1. **Regular Audits:** Periodically review user accounts and permissions.
2. **Use Groups:** Assign permissions to groups rather than individual users for easier management.
3. **Enforce Principle of Least Privilege:** Grant users only the permissions they need.
4. **Document Changes:** Maintain logs of changes to permissions or user accounts.
5. **Backup Configurations:** Backup files like /etc/passwd, /etc/shadow, and /etc/group regularly.

User and Group Management

Commands for Managing Users and Groups

Creating Users:

```
useradd <username>
```

Modifying Users:

```
usermod -aG <group> <username>
```

Creating Groups:

```
groupadd <groupname>
```

Assigning Groups:

```
usermod -g <groupname> <username>
```

Example: Create a user developer and add them to the webdev group:

```
useradd developer
usermod -aG webdev developer
```

Managing System Users vs. Regular Users

Differences

1. **System Users:** Used for system processes and services (e.g., root, www-data). Typically have UIDs below 1000.
2. **Regular Users:** Created for human users. Typically have UIDs starting from 1000.

Best Practices

- Avoid modifying system user accounts unless necessary.
- Ensure system users have minimal permissions for enhanced security.

Tip: Use the /etc/login.defs file to configure UID ranges for regular users and system users.

Password Policies and Security

Enforcing Password Policies

Minimum Length and Complexity:

```
passwd -n 8 <username>
```

  - o   Requires a minimum of 8 characters for the password.

Password Expiration:

```
chage -M 90 <username>
```

  - o   Forces password change every 90 days.

Lock Accounts After Inactivity:

```
usermod -L <username>
```

Best Practice: Use PAM (Pluggable Authentication Modules) to enforce complex password policies.

Common Pitfalls in Permission Management

Checklist to Avoid Mistakes

1. Granting excessive permissions (e.g., chmod 777).
2. Forgetting to apply recursive permissions with chmod −R.
3. Overlooking inherited group permissions.
4. Changing ownership of system-critical files.

Tip: Always test permission changes in a safe environment before applying to production.

File and Directory Ownership Management

Setting Ownership

Change Owner:

```
chown user:group file.txt
```

Set Default Group Ownership:

```
chmod g+s <directory>
```

- Ensures new files inherit the group of the parent directory.

Real-Life Example: Use group ownership and sticky bits for shared directories to control file access.

Advanced Access Control Techniques

Using ACLs for Granular Permissions

Set Permissions:

```
setfacl -m u:username:rwx file.txt
```
View ACLs:

```
getfacl file.txt
```

Tip: ACLs allow precise control over access for specific users or groups without altering the global permissions.

Automation for User Management

Create Multiple Users:

```
for user in user1 user2 user3; do
  useradd $user
  echo "password" | passwd --stdin $user
```

Set Group Permissions:

```
find /shared -type d -exec chmod g+s {} \;
```

Using Tools like Ansible

Automate user management across multiple systems:
- name: Create users

user:
  name: "{{ item }}"
  state: present
loop:
  - user1
  - user2

> **Best Practice:** Use automation tools to ensure consistency
> and reduce manual errors.

Summary and Glossary

Key Takeaways

- Proper management of user accounts and permissions is essential for security and functionality.
- Tools like passwd, chmod, chown, and ACLs allow fine-grained control over access.

- Automation simplifies and standardizes user and permission management.

Glossary

Term	Definition
passwd	Command to change or reset user passwords.
chmod	Modifies file and directory permissions.
chown	Changes ownership of files and directories.
ACL	Access Control List for granular permission control.
faillog	Displays failed login attempts and account status.
sshd_config	Configuration file for the SSH daemon.
PAM	Pluggable Authentication Modules for authentication policies.

Chapter 11: Security and Intrusion Detection

This chapter will teach you how to detect unauthorized access, monitor for suspicious activity, and troubleshoot security tools in a Linux system. You will also learn how to respond to security incidents, isolate affected systems, and analyze potential malware.

Security is a top concern in Linux systems, especially when it comes to detecting intrusions and unauthorized access. By understanding how to monitor system logs, configure firewalls, and use intrusion detection systems (IDS/IPS), you can secure your system. This chapter will provide you with practical tools and techniques for maintaining a secure Linux environment.

> **Real-Life Application:** If your system is compromised or under attack, this chapter will help you detect, respond, and recover from the security incident.

> **Note:** Regular security monitoring and updates are essential for preventing system breaches.

> **Warning:** Failing to monitor logs or configure security tools properly can leave your system vulnerable to attacks.

The Role of Security and Intrusion Detection in System Administration

Core Functions

1. **System Security Monitoring:** One of the primary roles of a system administrator is ensuring that the system is protected from unauthorized access and potential breaches.
2. **Why It Matters:** A breach in security can compromise sensitive data, cause system instability, and lead to severe reputational damage. Proactive monitoring and troubleshooting are essential to avoid these issues.

3. **Problem-Solving:** Troubleshooting security issues involves detecting unauthorized access, reviewing logs for unusual activity, configuring security tools like firewalls and IDS/IPS, and ensuring your system's policies are correct.

Key Characteristics of Troubleshooting Security and Intrusion Detection Issues

Characteristic	Importance
Log Monitoring	Detects suspicious activity like failed logins or unauthorized changes.
Firewalls and IDS/IPS	Blocks malicious traffic and prevents intrusions.
SELinux/AppArmor	Prevents unauthorized access by enforcing strict policies.
Incident Response	Isolates affected systems and restores them from backups.
Tools	Tools like fail2ban, iptables, and chkrootkit are essential for troubleshooting security issues.

Note: Security and intrusion detection require continuous monitoring and proactive measures to maintain system integrity.

Network Traffic Analysis

Tools for Network Analysis

1. **Wireshark:** A graphical tool for inspecting network packets.

tcpdump: A command-line utility for capturing and analyzing packets in real time.

```
tcpdump -i eth0
```

Real-Life Example

Scenario: Unexpected Outbound Connections

- A web server shows unusually high outbound traffic.

Use tcpdump to capture packets on the network interface:

```
tcpdump -i eth0 port 80
```

- Analyze the output to identify unauthorized data exfiltration.

  Warning: Ensure packet analysis tools are used responsibly, as they can expose sensitive data in network traffic.

Proactive Security Measures

Regular Updates

Update Packages: Use tools like apt or yum to keep the system and software up to date.

```
apt-get update && apt-get upgrade
```

Vulnerability Scanning

Use tools like **Lynis** or **OpenVAS** to identify system vulnerabilities.
 lynis audit system

> **Real-Life Example:** Running **Lynis** on a production server
> reveals misconfigured file permissions and outdated
> packages, which are promptly addressed.

> **Warning:** Neglecting updates leaves your system exposed to
> security flaws.

User and Process Monitoring

Tools

htop: An interactive process viewer.

ps: Lists running processes.
 ps aux | grep suspicious_process

Real-Life Example

Scenario: Unauthorized Cryptocurrency Mining

- The system slows down unexpectedly.
- Use htop to identify a process consuming high CPU resources.

Kill the suspicious process and investigate further:

```
kill -9 <PID>
```

> **Note:** Regularly check for unfamiliar processes to detect
> potential compromises.

Secure SSH Practices

Recommendations

Disable Root Login:

PermitRootLogin no

Use Key-Based Authentication:

```
ssh-keygen -t rsa -b 4096
```

Change Default Port:

Port 2222

Real-Life Example

Scenario: Brute-Force SSH Attack

- Logs reveal multiple failed SSH login attempts from the same IP.
- Mitigation:
    - Change the default port.
    - Enable fail2ban to block the attacker.

    Warning: Always keep backup copies of SSH keys to avoid being locked out of the system.

Incident Response Plan (IRP)

Steps in an IRP

1. **Detection:** Identify and confirm the incident.

Containment: Isolate affected systems to prevent further spread.

ifdown eth0

2. **Eradication:** Remove the cause of the incident (e.g., malware).
3. **Recovery:** Restore from clean backups and validate the system.

4. **Lessons Learned:** Document the incident to improve future responses.

Real-Life Example

Scenario: Compromised Database Server

- Detection: The database server is unresponsive, and logs indicate unauthorized queries.
- Containment: Disconnect the server from the network.
- Eradication: Identify and remove the malicious script.
- Recovery: Restore the database from a backup taken before the compromise.
- Document the attack to improve security policies.

   Note: An IRP ensures a structured and effective response to security incidents.

Encryption and Secure Communication

Tools

GPG: Encrypt files and emails.

```
gpg -c filename
```
1. **OpenSSL:** Generate SSL certificates for secure web communication.

Real-Life Example

Scenario: Encrypting Configuration Files

Sensitive configuration files are encrypted using GPG:

```
gpg -c config.conf
```
- Decryption is restricted to authorized administrators.

Warning: Ensure encrypted files are securely stored and keys are not misplaced.

Backup and Disaster Recovery

Backup Strategies

Automate Backups: Use tools like rsnapshot or cron.
rsync -av /source /backup

1. **Test Backups:** Regularly verify the integrity of backups.

Real-Life Example

Scenario: Ransomware Attack

- Files on the server are encrypted, and a ransom note appears.
- Mitigation:
    - Disconnect the server from the network.
    - Restore files from a recent, verified backup.

Note: Store backups offsite to protect against local disasters.

Warning: Unverified backups may fail during recovery.

Real-Life Scenarios and Challenges

Scenario 1: Ransomware Attack

1. **Detection:** Files are encrypted and demand for payment appears.
2. **Response:**
    - Disconnect the affected system from the network.
    - Use backups to restore files.
    - Investigate the source of the attack.

Scenario 2: DDoS Attack

1. **Detection:** Unusual traffic overwhelms the system.
2. **Response:**

Use rate-limiting in iptables to mitigate traffic.
iptables -A INPUT -p tcp --dport 80 -m limit --limit 25/minute --limit-burst 100 -j ACCEPT

   o Contact your hosting provider for additional support.

   Note: Simulating these scenarios can improve your readiness for real attacks.

Security Best Practices Checklist

1. **Regular Updates:** Keep the system and software updated.
2. **Monitor Logs:** Use tools like Logwatch for centralized log monitoring.
3. **Harden SSH:** Disable root login, use key-based authentication, and change the default port.
4. **Use IDS/IPS:** Deploy tools like Snort or Suricata to monitor traffic.
5. **Encrypt Sensitive Data:** Use GPG or OpenSSL for encryption.
6. **Automate Backups:** Schedule regular, automated backups.
7. **Test Recovery Plans:** Ensure backups and disaster recovery plans are effective.
8. **Train Staff:** Educate users and administrators on security best practices.

   Warning: Neglecting any of these practices can significantly increase the risk of a security breach.

Summary and Glossary

Key Takeaways

- Proactive security measures like log monitoring and firewalls are essential for detecting and preventing intrusions.
- Tools like fail2ban, chkrootkit, iptables, and SELinux help protect systems from unauthorized access.
- Incident response requires isolating affected systems, analyzing malware, and restoring from backups.

Glossary

Term	Definition
fail2ban	Blocks IPs after repeated failed login attempts.
iptables	Configures IP packet filtering rules.
chkrootkit	Scans for rootkits in the system.
SELinux	Security-Enhanced Linux for mandatory access control.
AppArmor	Restricts applications to specific resources.
audit2allow	Generates SELinux policies for denied actions.
IDS/IPS	Intrusion Detection/Prevention Systems to monitor and block malicious traffic.

Chapter 12: Troubleshooting Storage and Backups

This chapter will guide you through diagnosing storage device issues, troubleshooting backup failures, and verifying backup integrity in a Linux system. You will also learn how to resolve common issues related to cloud storage services and ensure that your backup processes are running smoothly.

Data storage and backups are essential for system reliability and data protection. When storage devices fail or backups don't work correctly, it can lead to significant data loss or system downtime. This chapter covers common tools and techniques to troubleshoot storage devices and backup issues.

> **Real-Life Application:** If your storage device fails, or you encounter backup failures, this chapter will teach you how to quickly identify the problem and take appropriate action to fix it.
>
> **Note:** Proactively monitoring storage and backups can help you catch issues before they become critical.
>
> **Warning:** Neglecting storage health or backup verification increases the risk of catastrophic data loss.

The Role of Troubleshooting Storage and Backup Issues

Why It Matters

1. **Foundation of Reliability:** Storage and backups are foundational elements of system administration.
2. **Data Security:** Ensuring that data is safely stored and backed up helps in maintaining system reliability and security.
3. **Critical Recovery:** If a backup failure or storage issue occurs, the ability to restore data or fix storage-related problems is essential.

Problem-Solving

1. **Storage Issues:** Diagnosing hardware problems, identifying drive failures, and ensuring proper connections.
2. **Backup Failures:** Troubleshooting backup tools, resolving permission issues, and debugging network-related backup problems.
3. **Recovery Assurance:** Regularly verifying backups ensures they are complete and usable during emergencies.

Key Characteristics of Troubleshooting Storage and Backup Issues

Area	Importance
Storage Devices	Diagnosing hardware failures and corrupted partitions.
Backup Failures	Identifying and fixing issues with backup tools or processes.
Backup Integrity	Ensuring backups are accurate and restorable.
Cloud Storage	Debugging issues with cloud-based backup services.

Note: Proactively monitoring storage health and backup success rates can prevent critical data loss.

Warning: Failing to address early signs of storage failure (e.g., SMART errors) may result in irreversible data loss.

Diagnosing Storage Device Issues

Common Storage Problems

1. **Failing Hard Drives:** Symptoms include unusual noises, slow response times, or frequent read/write errors.
2. **Corrupted Partitions:** Partitions may become unreadable due to filesystem corruption.
3. **Connection Problems:** Devices may not appear in the system if improperly connected.

Tools for Diagnosis

lsblk: Lists information about all available block devices.
lsblk

blkid: Displays information about block devices, including UUID and filesystem type.
 blkid

smartctl: Monitors storage device health using SMART technology.
 smartctl -a /dev/sda

> **Real-Life Example:** A server experiences intermittent disk errors. Running smartctl reveals several reallocated sectors, indicating impending failure. Replacing the disk prevents potential data loss.

> **Best Practice:** Regularly monitor disk health using SMART and replace failing drives before they fail completely.

Resolving Backup Failures

Common Causes of Backup Failures

1. **Insufficient Disk Space:** Backups fail when there isn't enough space in the destination.
2. **File Permission Issues:** Missing permissions can prevent files from being backed up.
3. **Network Connectivity Issues:** Interruptions during network-based backups can cause failures.

Tools and Techniques

Using rsync: A versatile tool for backups.

```
rsync -av --delete /source/ /destination/
```

1. **Debugging Scripts:** Ensure scripts have correct paths, permissions, and sufficient disk space.
2. **Checking Logs:** Review logs to identify specific errors causing the failure.

   Real-Life Example: A backup script fails due to permission issues. Adjusting file permissions with chmod resolves the problem, allowing the backup to complete successfully.

   Note: Automate backup success notifications to catch failures promptly.

   Warning: Always verify available disk space before running large backups to avoid mid-process failures.

Verifying Backup Integrity

Why It Matters

Verifying backup integrity ensures that backed-up data is complete, accurate, and restorable in case of emergencies.

Tools for Verification

Checksum Tools: Compare file checksums to verify integrity.
md5sum /path/to/file

sha256sum /path/to/file

Test Restores: Perform test restores periodically.
cp /backup/file /restored/

> **Real-Life Example:** A full backup completes successfully, but test restores reveal corrupted files. Revisiting the backup process and verifying integrity prevents future failures.

> **Best Practice:** Schedule periodic test restores to confirm backup integrity and usability.

> **Warning:** Relying on untested backups can lead to unexpected failures during emergencies.

Debugging Cloud Storage Services

Common Issues

1. **Authentication Failures:** Incorrect API keys or credentials can block backups.
2. **Network Problems:** Unreachable cloud services due to firewall or connectivity issues.
3. **Configuration Errors:** Misconfigured settings in cloud backup scripts.

Steps for Debugging

Verify Network and Credentials: Ensure the system can reach the cloud service and uses the correct credentials.
ping cloudservice.com

1. **Check Logs:** Review cloud-specific logs for error messages.
2. **Use Diagnostic Tools:** Utilize tools provided by cloud services to identify and resolve errors.

Real-Life Example: A cloud backup fails repeatedly. Reviewing logs shows API key expiration. Regenerating the key resolves the issue and restores functionality.

Best Practice: Use encrypted connections and secure credentials when configuring cloud backups.

Filesystem-Specific Issues

Troubleshooting Filesystems

ext4: Use fsck to check and repair errors.
fsck /dev/sda1

XFS: Use xfs_repair for XFS filesystems.
xfs_repair /dev/sda1

Real-Life Example: After a power outage, an ext4 partition fails to mount. Running fsck repairs inode errors, restoring access to data.

Warning: Always unmount a partition before performing filesystem repairs to avoid data corruption.

Storage Optimization

Trim SSDs: Use fstrim to improve SSD performance.
fstrim /mountpoint
Reclaim Space: Identify large files using du or ncdu.
du -sh /path

Best Practice: Regularly monitor and optimize storage usage to avoid running out of space.

Real-Life Example: Disk usage on a production server grows rapidly. Using du identifies large log files that are safely archived and deleted, freeing up space.

Note: Schedule automated trim operations for SSDs to maintain performance.

Automation for Backups

Automating Backup Processes

Using cron: Schedule regular backups.
 crontab -e

0 2 * * * rsync -av /source/ /backup/

1. **Using Tools:** Employ tools like Duplicity or Restic for automated and encrypted backups.
   Real-Life Example: Automating nightly incremental backups with cron ensures consistent data protection without manual intervention.
   Warning: Ensure automated backups include logs to identify failures.

Common Pitfalls in Storage and Backups

Avoid These Mistakes

1. **Neglecting Test Restores:** Backups are useless if they can't be restored.
2. **Ignoring SMART Warnings:** Early warning signs of drive failure should not be overlooked.

3. **Overwriting Backups:** Rotating backups prevent data loss from accidental overwrites.
   Real-Life Example: An organization realizes too late that backups are incomplete because test restores were never performed. Implementing periodic restore tests avoids similar pitfalls.
   Note: Regularly review backup logs and test restores to catch issues early.

Summary and Glossary

1. Troubleshooting storage and backup issues requires understanding tools like lsblk, blkid, smartctl, and rsync.
2. Verifying backups is as important as creating them. Regular test restores ensure reliability.

Glossary

Term	Definition
rsync	A command-line tool for file synchronization and backup.
smartctl	A tool for monitoring the health of storage devices using SMART.
md5sum	Generates and verifies MD5 checksums for file integrity.
Backup Integrity	Ensuring backups are complete and restorable.

Note: Always maintain a proactive approach to monitoring and testing your storage and backup solutions to minimize risks and ensure system reliability.

Chapter 13: Automating Troubleshooting Tasks

This chapter focuses on automating common troubleshooting tasks using scripting and monitoring tools. By automating diagnostics, log analysis, and issue alerts, system administrators can proactively address problems before they impact the system or users.

Automating troubleshooting helps reduce the time spent on manual tasks, ensures consistency, and allows for proactive monitoring of systems. By using tools like Bash, Python, and integrating with monitoring platforms, administrators can automate repetitive troubleshooting tasks, such as system health checks, log analysis, and sending alerts when problems arise.

> **Real-Life Application:** Imagine a scenario where your server's disk usage exceeds a threshold, or memory usage is high. By automating these checks, you can receive alerts and take action before these issues cause downtime.

The Role of Automating Troubleshooting Tasks

Why It Matters

1. **Time Efficiency:** Automation saves time by handling repetitive tasks, freeing administrators for higher-level problem-solving.
2. **Consistency:** Automated processes reduce human error and ensure regular system checks.
3. **Proactive Problem-Solving:** Automated alerts allow for quicker responses to potential system failures.

Problem-Solving

1. **Diagnostics:** Automating system health checks reduces manual troubleshooting time.
2. **Alerts and Notifications:** Proactively addressing warnings ensures minimal impact on users.
3. **Recovery:** Automated recovery scripts help maintain uptime and resolve common failures quickly.

Note: Proactive automation can prevent minor issues from escalating into critical system failures.

Key Characteristics of Automating Troubleshooting Tasks

Characteristic	Importance
Scripting	Automates repetitive tasks like log parsing and disk checks.
Scheduling	Ensures regular execution of diagnostics and maintenance tasks.
Alerting	Notifies administrators of critical issues in real-time.
Monitoring Integration	Provides a centralized view of system health and performance.

Warning: Poorly written scripts or misconfigured automation can create more problems than they solve. Always test your automation thoroughly.

Writing Scripts for Common Issues

Bash Scripts

Bash scripts are widely used for automating simple system tasks like file management, diagnostics, and log analysis.

Example: Disk Space Checker

```bash
#!/bin/bash
echo "Checking disk space..."
df -h | grep -v 'tmpfs'
```

Python Scripts

Python is a powerful language for more complex tasks, such as interacting with APIs, analyzing logs, or integrating with monitoring tools.

Example: CPU Usage Monitor

```python
import psutil
cpu_usage = psutil.cpu_percent(interval=1)
if cpu_usage > 80:
    print(f"Warning: CPU usage is high at {cpu_usage}%")
else:
    print(f"CPU usage is normal: {cpu_usage}%")
```

> **Real-Life Example:** A company uses Bash scripts to monitor disk space and Python scripts to check memory usage, ensuring consistent resource availability.

> **Best Practice:** Modularize your scripts to make them reusable and easier to debug.

Real-Life Troubleshooting Scenarios

Example 1: Automating Service Restart

A critical web server service fails sporadically. Instead of manually restarting it each time, an administrator writes a script to monitor the service and restart it automatically if it stops:

Service Monitor Script

```bash
#!/bin/bash
if ! systemctl is-active --quiet apache2; then
    echo "Apache2 service is down. Restarting..."
    systemctl restart apache2
fi
```

Example 2: Daily Health Report

A daily script generates a report summarizing disk usage, memory usage, and CPU load, emailing it to the system administrator:

Health Report Script

```bash
#!/bin/bash
echo "Daily System Health Report" > /tmp/report.txt
df -h >> /tmp/report.txt
free -h >> /tmp/report.txt
top -bn1 | head -10 >> /tmp/report.txt
mail -s "System Health Report" admin@example.com < /tmp/report.txt
```

Note: These automated scripts help prevent downtime by addressing recurring issues proactively.

Version Control for Automation Scripts

Why Version Control Matters

1. **Tracking Changes:** Version control allows you to track changes to scripts, making it easier to troubleshoot when issues arise.
2. **Collaboration:** Enables multiple team members to work on the same scripts without conflicts.
3. **Rollback:** Provides the ability to revert to a previous version if a change introduces bugs.

Using Git for Script Management

Initialize a Git Repository:
```
git init
```

Track Changes to Scripts:
```
git add script.sh

git commit -m "Initial commit of troubleshooting script"
```

View History:
```
git log
```

> **Best Practice:** Always use meaningful commit messages to document changes.

Scheduling Automated Diagnostics

Using Cron

cron is a time-based job scheduler that runs tasks automatically at specified intervals.

Example: Daily Disk Space Check at 3:00 AM

0 3 * * * /path/to/disk_check_script.sh

Using systemd Timers

systemd timers provide more flexibility and integration into modern Linux systems.

Example: Hourly System Health Check

Timer Configuration

[Unit]

Description=Run system health check hourly

[Timer]

OnCalendar=hourly

[Install]

WantedBy=timers.target

Service Configuration

[Unit]

Description=System health check service

[Service]

ExecStart=/path/to/system_health_check.sh

> **Real-Life Example:** Scheduling periodic checks ensures you catch issues like disk overuse or high CPU load before they escalate.

> **Warning:** Misconfigured schedules may lead to excessive resource usage or missed checks.

Automating Log Analysis

Parsing Logs with Scripts

Automate log parsing to identify errors, failed login attempts, or service failures.

Example: Failed Login Detector

```
#!/bin/bash
grep 'Failed password' /var/log/auth.log > /path/to/failed_logins.log
echo "Failed login attempts logged."
```

Using grep, awk, and sed

These tools are invaluable for filtering and analyzing logs.

Example: List Users with Failed Logins

grep "Failed password" /var/log/auth.log | awk '{print $9}' | sort | uniq -c

Real-Life Example: Automated log analysis scripts generate daily reports of suspicious activity, helping administrators identify potential security threats.

Best Practice: Use centralized log management tools to consolidate and analyze logs from multiple systems.

Best Practices for Alert Management

Avoid Alert Fatigue

1. **Prioritize Alerts:** Categorize alerts by severity (e.g., critical, warning, informational).
2. **Threshold Tuning:** Set thresholds that align with your environment to avoid unnecessary alerts.
3. **Batch Notifications:** Group similar alerts to reduce noise.

Tools for Managing Alerts

- **PagerDuty:** Escalation and incident management.
- **Slack Integration:** Send alerts to specific Slack channels for better visibility.

Real-Life Example: A server generates hundreds of alerts during a high CPU load event. By prioritizing critical alerts, the administrator focuses on the root cause rather than the noise.

Performance Monitoring Dashboards

Tools for Visual Monitoring

1. **Grafana:** Create dashboards to visualize system metrics.
2. **Kibana:** Analyze and visualize log data from the Elastic Stack.
3. **Zabbix Dashboards:** Provide a comprehensive view of monitored systems.

Example: Grafana Dashboard for Resource Monitoring

- **Metrics Monitored:**
    - CPU Usage
    - Memory Usage
    - Disk I/O
    - Network Traffic
- **Alert Integration:** Set up alerts in Grafana for metrics exceeding thresholds.
  Real-Life Example: A Grafana dashboard highlights a spike in disk I/O during peak hours, prompting the administrator to optimize database queries.
  Best Practice: Regularly update dashboards to include new metrics as your environment evolves.

Integrating with Monitoring Tools

Popular Tools for Automation

Tool	Features
Nagios	Tracks system and service health.
Zabbix	Enterprise-class monitoring and alerting.
Prometheus	Collects metrics and integrates with alerting systems.

Real-Life Example: Integrating Prometheus with Grafana provides a visual representation of system health, making it easier to spot trends and anomalies.

Best Practice: Combine monitoring tools with automated scripts for comprehensive troubleshooting coverage.

Summary and Glossary

Key Takeaways

1. Automating troubleshooting tasks reduces manual effort and ensures proactive system monitoring.
2. Use tools like Bash, Python, cron, and monitoring platforms to automate diagnostics, log analysis, and alerting.
3. Regularly review and refine automation scripts to ensure they remain effective and relevant.

Glossary

Term	Definition
Bash	A shell scripting language for system automation.
Python	A versatile programming language used for complex automation tasks.
cron	A time-based job scheduler for Unix-like systems.
Nagios	A monitoring tool for infrastructure and service health.
Promethe us	A monitoring toolkit designed for reliability and scalability.

Note: Automation is a powerful tool but must be implemented thoughtfully to avoid introducing new risks or inefficiencies.

Chapter 14: Performance Troubleshooting

This chapter will cover how to diagnose and troubleshoot performance issues on Linux systems, focusing on tools and techniques to identify bottlenecks, and fine-tune system performance. Performance issues often manifest as slow response times, high CPU usage, or memory shortages. This chapter aims to equip you with the skills to identify the cause of these problems and optimize system performance.

Performance troubleshooting involves diagnosing resource limitations, system bottlenecks, and optimizing kernel and application parameters. Tools like perf, iotop, sar, and others provide insight into where resources are being used inefficiently or where bottlenecks occur.

> **Real-Life Application:** If your web server is slow, understanding where the bottleneck is (whether it's CPU, memory, I/O, or network) and how to resolve it is crucial for improving response times and overall system performance.

The Role of Performance Troubleshooting

Why It Matters

1. **System Stability:** Performance issues can lead to delays, application crashes, and even downtime.
2. **User Satisfaction:** Optimized performance ensures better user experience with faster response times.
3. **Resource Efficiency:** Proper troubleshooting helps identify underutilized or overutilized resources, allowing better allocation and optimization.

Problem-Solving

1. **Resource Bottlenecks:** Identify whether issues stem from CPU, memory, disk, or network constraints.
2. **Optimization:** Fine-tune kernel parameters, adjust application configurations, and improve resource utilization.
3. **Recovery:** Quickly pinpoint performance degradation causes and apply targeted fixes.

Key Characteristics of Performance Troubleshooting

Characteristic	Importance
Resource Utilization	Monitor CPU, memory, disk I/O, and network usage.
Bottleneck Identification	Identify whether issues are CPU, memory, I/O, or network-bound.
System Tuning	Fine-tune kernel and application settings for optimal performance.
Profiling	Use tools to gather real-time performance data.

Warning: Misdiagnosing performance issues can lead to unnecessary downtime or inefficient fixes. Use tools effectively to pinpoint exact causes.

Real-Life Troubleshooting Scenarios

Scenario 1: Slow Database Performance

Symptom: Queries are taking significantly longer to execute. **Solution:**

1. Use iotop to check for high disk I/O usage.
2. Use strace to monitor system calls and identify excessive file reads/writes.
3. Optimize queries and add indexes to reduce execution time.

Scenario 2: High CPU Usage on Application Server

Symptom: Application server becomes unresponsive under heavy load. **Solution:**

1. Use top or perf to identify processes consuming high CPU.
2. Fine-tune application thread or connection limits to optimize resource allocation.
3. Adjust kernel parameters like fs.file-max to handle more simultaneous connections.

Scenario 3: Network Latency in Web Applications

Symptom: Users experience slow loading times. **Solution:**

1. Use ping and iperf to test network latency and bandwidth.
2. Use tcpdump to analyze packet loss or delayed responses.
3. Optimize web server configurations, such as enabling compression or caching.

   Note: Real-life scenarios often involve a combination of factors; using multiple tools together provides a clearer picture of the problem.

Best Practices for Performance Monitoring

1. **Implement Regular Monitoring:**

   - Use tools like Nagios, Zabbix, or Prometheus for continuous monitoring of system metrics.
   - Set up dashboards in Grafana for visual insights into performance trends.

2. **Establish Baselines:**

   - Understand normal system behavior to detect anomalies more effectively.
   - Example: Record average CPU and memory usage during typical workloads.

3. **Automate Alerts:**

   - Configure alerts for critical metrics, such as CPU exceeding 90% or disk space dropping below 20%.
   - Use tools like Alertmanager for automated notifications.

4. **Regularly Test Configurations:**

   - Periodically stress-test your system to identify potential bottlenecks under load.

5. **Document Performance Metrics:**

   - Maintain logs of historical performance metrics to identify trends and plan capacity upgrades.

Best Practice: Regular monitoring helps detect performance degradation early, preventing it from escalating into critical issues.

Network Performance Troubleshooting

Common Network Issues

1. **High Latency:** Increased delay in data transfer.
   - **Tool:** Use ping to measure response times.
2. **Packet Loss:** Missing data packets during transmission.
   - **Tool:** Use tcpdump to capture and analyze network traffic.
3. **Bandwidth Bottlenecks:** Insufficient network capacity causing slow transfers.
   - **Tool:** Use iperf to measure throughput.

Tools and Techniques

iftop: Real-time bandwidth usage per connection.
 sudo iftop

netstat: Displays network connections, routing tables, and statistics.
 netstat -i

iperf: Measures maximum achievable bandwidth.
 iperf -c <server_address>

> **Real-Life Example:** A file transfer between servers is slow. Using iperf reveals limited bandwidth, prompting a network configuration update to improve throughput.

Checklist for Performance Troubleshooting

Step-by-Step Approach

1. **Identify Symptoms:**
   - Note specific issues (e.g., slow response times, high CPU usage).
2. **Gather Metrics:**

- Use tools like top, iotop, sar, and vmstat to collect relevant data.
3. **Analyze Bottlenecks:**
   - Determine whether the issue is CPU, memory, disk I/O, or network-related.
4. **Apply Fixes:**
   - Adjust kernel parameters, optimize applications, or resolve resource conflicts.
5. **Monitor Results:**
   - Reassess system performance after applying changes.
6. **Document Findings:**
   - Record the issue, solution, and any system changes for future reference.

Best Practice: Follow this checklist systematically to ensure thorough troubleshooting and resolution.

Common Pitfalls in Performance Tuning

1. **Over-Optimizing:**
   - Tweaking parameters without understanding the full impact can destabilize the system.
2. **Ignoring Baselines:**
   - Failure to establish performance baselines makes it harder to identify anomalies.
3. **Neglecting Logs:**
   - Overlooking logs can lead to missed opportunities for diagnosing underlying issues.
4. **Skipping Testing:**
   - Implementing changes without testing them in a staging environment risks introducing new problems.
5. **Uncoordinated Changes:**

   - Making multiple adjustments simultaneously can obscure the actual cause of improvements or regressions.

Warning: Avoid rushing to implement changes without a clear understanding of their impact. Always test adjustments in a controlled environment.

Summary and Glossary

1. Performance troubleshooting involves identifying and resolving resource bottlenecks.
2. Tools like perf, iotop, and sar provide critical insights into system performance.
3. Fine-tuning kernel and application parameters optimizes resource usage and improves response times.

Glossary

Term	Definition
Bottleneck	A resource constraint that limits overall performance.
perf	A tool for analyzing performance at the process/kernel level.
iotop	A real-time disk I/O monitoring tool.
sar	A system activity reporting tool for Linux.
strace	A tool for tracing system calls made by a process.

Note: Regular monitoring and proactive performance tuning are essential for maintaining system stability and user satisfaction.

Chapter 15: Virtualization and Container Troubleshooting

This chapter focuses on troubleshooting virtualized environments and containers in Linux systems. With the increasing adoption of virtualization technologies (like VMs) and containers (like Docker and Kubernetes), understanding how to identify and resolve issues in these environments is crucial for maintaining system stability and performance.

Virtual machines (VMs) and containers provide a way to isolate applications and services, but they come with their own set of challenges. Common issues include resource overcommitment, misconfigurations in the hypervisor, and problems specific to containerized applications. This chapter will equip you with the tools and techniques to diagnose and troubleshoot these issues.

> **Real-Life Application:** If you're running a web application inside a container and it suddenly becomes unresponsive, understanding how to use tools like `docker stats` or `virt-top` will help you pinpoint the issue—whether it's resource starvation, misconfigurations, or container crashes.

The Role of Virtualization and Container Troubleshooting

Why It Matters

1. **Resource Efficiency:** Virtualization and containers allow systems to run multiple isolated applications and services on the same hardware.
2. **Stability:** Mismanagement of virtual resources can lead to degraded performance, system crashes, or application failures.
3. **Scalability:** Proper troubleshooting ensures that virtual environments scale effectively without introducing bottlenecks or resource contention.

Problem-Solving

1. **Resource Management:** Diagnose and resolve resource allocation issues to avoid performance bottlenecks.
2. **Configuration Optimization:** Ensure hypervisors and containers are correctly configured to meet workload requirements.
3. **Recovery:** Quickly identify and fix issues to minimize downtime and maintain service availability.

Key Characteristics of Virtualization and Container Troubleshooting

Characteristic	Importance
Resource Overcommitment	Avoid allocating more resources than physically available.
Isolation	Containers isolate applications, but misconfigurations can still affect performance.
Monitoring Tools	Specialized tools help track resource usage in virtual environments.
Networking	Properly configuring virtual and container networking is crucial for performance.

Warning: Misconfigured virtualization settings or container limits can lead to significant performance degradation or system instability.

Real-Life Troubleshooting Scenarios

Scenario 1: Kubernetes Pod Crash

Symptom: A Kubernetes pod continuously crashes due to an unresponsive database connection. **Solution:**

1. Use kubectl logs to check for database connection errors.
2. Reconfigure database parameters and verify connectivity using ping or telnet from the pod.
3. Restart the pod to confirm the fix.

Scenario 2: VM Disk I/O Bottleneck

Symptom: A virtual machine slows down during peak hours due to insufficient disk I/O. **Solution:**

1. Use iostat to identify high I/O wait times.
2. Allocate dedicated storage resources or increase IOPS limits for the VM.
3. Migrate storage to higher-performance disks if needed.

Scenario 3: Docker Container Environment Issue

Symptom: A Docker container fails to start due to a missing environment variable. **Solution:**

1. Use docker inspect to review the container's environment settings.
2. Add the missing environment variable using docker run -e.
3. Restart the container and validate its operation.

Advanced Tools for Virtualization and Containers

Tool	Purpose
Vagrant	Manage and replicate virtualized development environments.
Podman	Lightweight container management without requiring a daemon.
Prometheus with cAdvisor	Monitor container performance and visualize trends.

Note: Use these tools in combination with standard Linux utilities for a comprehensive troubleshooting approach.

Best Practices for Resource Allocation

1. **Avoid Overcommitment:**
   - Ensure resource requests do not exceed physical limits.
   - Use Kubernetes resource quotas and limits for better control.
2. **Set Container Limits:**
   - Use docker run --memory or docker run --cpus to limit container resource usage.
3. **Pin Critical Resources:**
   - Pin critical VMs to specific CPU cores for predictable performance.
   - Allocate dedicated memory for high-priority containers or VMs.

4. **Monitor Usage Trends:**
   o Regularly review resource utilization with tools like virt-top or docker stats to identify trends and optimize allocations.

Networking in Virtualized Environments

Common Issues

1. **IP Conflicts:** Virtual machines or containers may share overlapping IP ranges.
2. **Misconfigured Bridges:** Virtual bridges may not forward traffic correctly.
3. **Packet Loss:** High traffic or misconfigured routes can cause dropped packets.

Tools for Networking Debugging

bridge-utils: Debug and manage virtual bridges.
brctl show

ip commands: Inspect and configure network interfaces.
ip a

ip r

tcpdump: Analyze packet flows.
tcpdump -i eth0

> **Real-Life Example:** A VM loses connectivity due to a misconfigured virtual bridge. Using bridge-utils, you identify the problem and reconfigure the bridge for proper routing.

Security Considerations

1. **Container Security:**
   - Use namespaces and seccomp profiles to limit container permissions.
   - Regularly scan containers with tools like **Trivy** to identify vulnerabilities.
2. **Hypervisor Hardening:**
   - Enable SELinux or AppArmor to restrict access to hypervisor files.
   - Update hypervisor software regularly to patch security vulnerabilities.
3. **Network Security:**
   - Use firewalls to isolate virtual machines and container networks.
   - Monitor for unauthorized access using intrusion detection systems (IDS).

Warning: Failing to secure containers or hypervisors can expose your systems to serious vulnerabilities.

Common Pitfalls in Virtualization and Containers

1. **Improper Resource Limits:** Not setting memory or CPU limits can lead to resource contention and instability.
2. **Neglecting Logs:** Logs provide critical insights but are often overlooked.
3. **Skipping Updates:** Running outdated container images or hypervisor versions can lead to security and performance issues.
4. **Uncoordinated Changes:** Making changes without proper testing can introduce new problems.
   Best Practice: Always test changes in a staging environment before applying them to production systems.

Checklist for Virtualization and Container Troubleshooting

General Steps

1. **Verify Resource Allocation:**
   - Use `virt-top` for VMs and `docker stats` for containers to monitor usage.
2. **Check Logs:**
   - Use `docker logs`, `kubectl logs`, or hypervisor logs to identify issues.
3. **Test Configurations:**
   - Validate networking, storage, and CPU/memory allocations.
4. **Apply Fixes:**
   - Adjust resource limits, reconfigure virtual networks, or optimize storage settings.
5. **Monitor Results:**
   - Observe system performance post-fix to ensure stability.

Performance Optimization Tips

1. **Reduce Latency:**
   - Use overlay networks sparingly to avoid additional routing overhead.
2. **Optimize Disk Usage:**
   - Preallocate disk space for VM images using `qemu-img`.
3. **Enable Caching:**
   - Use caching mechanisms in containers to minimize repetitive I/O operations.
   Real-Life Example: After noticing high latency in containerized workloads, switching to host-based networking and enabling caching improved response times

significantly.

Summary and Glossary

Key Takeaways:

- Troubleshooting virtualization and containers requires specialized tools and techniques.
- Resource overcommitment, hypervisor misconfigurations, and container issues are common challenges.

Glossary:

Term	Definition
Resource Overcommitment	Allocating more resources than physically available on the host.
Hypervisor	Software that creates and manages virtual machines.
virt-top	A tool for real-time monitoring of virtual machine performance.
docker stats	Command for monitoring Docker container resource usage.
cAdvisor	A monitoring tool for container performance metrics.

Note: Proper resource allocation and monitoring are critical for maintaining stable and efficient virtualized and containerized environments.

Chapter 16: Advanced Troubleshooting Scenarios

This chapter explores advanced troubleshooting techniques for complex systems. You will learn how to troubleshoot issues that span multiple systems, handle failures in distributed environments, and resolve rare or intermittent problems. By leveraging centralized logging, trace logs, and system snapshots, you can enhance your troubleshooting skills for large, complicated environments.

Modern systems are often distributed, with multiple machines working together to deliver a service. Troubleshooting in such environments requires unique tools and techniques. This chapter provides the knowledge needed to approach these scenarios effectively, including real-life case studies to illustrate how advanced techniques are applied.

> **Real-Life Application:** If your company's distributed database system experiences random slowdowns across regions, this chapter will show you how to diagnose the root cause—whether it's network latency, misconfigured load balancers, or intermittent server failures—using tools like centralized logs and trace logs.

The Role of Advanced Troubleshooting

Why It Matters

1. **Complexity:** Distributed systems introduce multi-layered challenges requiring sophisticated tools and methods.
2. **Efficiency:** Advanced troubleshooting reduces downtime and ensures smooth operations in large-scale environments.
3. **Precision:** Gathering and correlating data across systems allows pinpointing issues faster and with greater accuracy.

Problem-Solving

- **Data Gathering:** Use centralized logs, snapshots, and monitoring tools to collect relevant data.
- **Correlating Information:** Analyze data across multiple systems to identify root causes.
- **Applying Solutions:** Use specialized tools and methods to fix problems and prevent recurrences.

Recovery

Effective techniques reduce the time required to diagnose and recover from system failures, especially in scenarios involving intermittent or hard-to-replicate issues.

Key Characteristics of Advanced Troubleshooting

Characteristic	Importance
Multi-System Involvement	Problems often arise from interactions between systems.
Centralized Logging	Aggregates logs for unified analysis across systems.
Intermittent Issues	Captures hard-to-reproduce problems with detailed logs.
Complexity	Requires familiarity with diverse tools and techniques.

Note: Centralized logging and proactive monitoring are essential for managing complex distributed environments.

Multi-System Debugging

Problem Overview

When troubleshooting distributed systems, gathering data from multiple sources is critical. Problems often involve interactions among servers, network devices, and cloud resources.

Symptoms

- A web application works for some users but fails for others.
- Performance degradation due to server misconfigurations or load balancer issues.

Solution

1. Collect logs from all involved systems using a centralized logging system (e.g., ELK Stack, Splunk).
2. Correlate events across systems by time-stamping log entries.
3. Use network monitoring tools (e.g., netstat, tcpdump) to identify connectivity issues.

   Real-Life Example: A cloud-based application shows inconsistent performance across regions. By analyzing traceroute outputs and centralized logs, the issue is traced to a network bottleneck between data centers.

Handling Distributed System Failures

Problem Overview

Failures in distributed systems can arise from network issues, misconfigured services, or application-level bugs. Isolating failures requires specialized tools and techniques.

Symptoms

- A database responds slowly or times out intermittently.
- Microservices fail to return data or experience delays.

Solution

1. **Monitoring Tools:** Use Prometheus or Nagios to track system health and pinpoint failures.
2. **Centralized Logging:** View the request flow across services to identify where failures occur.
3. **Fault Tolerance:** Implement circuit breakers or retries to handle temporary failures.

   Real-Life Example: A microservices-based application suffers from intermittent database connection issues. By using docker stats and centralized logs, you identify a bottleneck caused by excessive resource consumption from another service.

Using Centralized Logging Systems

Problem Overview

Manually checking logs on multiple machines is inefficient in distributed environments. Centralized logging systems aggregate logs for easier analysis.

Symptoms

- Logs are too dispersed to analyze manually.
- Important trends or error patterns are missed due to scattered logs.

Solution

1. **Set Up Centralized Logging:** Use tools like ELK Stack, Splunk, or Fluentd.
2. **Query and Dashboards:** Identify trends, errors, or patterns across systems.
3. **Correlate Logs:** Match logs based on timestamps to trace issues.

   Real-Life Example: After setting up an ELK stack, a spike in error messages is noticed in a specific service. Examining correlated logs across systems reveals a configuration issue causing the problem.

Resolving Rare and Intermittent Issues

Problem Overview

Sporadic or conditional issues are challenging to reproduce and diagnose.

Symptoms

- Errors occur randomly or only under heavy load.
- No clear cause is visible in standard logs.

Solution

1. **Trace Logs:** Use strace or ltrace to capture system and library calls.
2. **System Snapshots:** Record CPU, memory, and I/O states during failures.
3. **Detailed Logging:** Increase verbosity in logs to capture additional context.

Real-Life Example: A server crashes sporadically. Using dmesg logs and system snapshots, the issue is identified as a faulty kernel module under heavy load.

Using Trace Logs and System Snapshots

Problem Overview

Trace logs and system snapshots provide detailed insights into system behavior during failures.

Symptoms

- Missing context for failures.
- Issues occur under specific conditions (e.g., high load or off-peak hours).

Solution

Trace Logs: Use tools like strace to track system calls.

```
strace -p <pid>
```

System Snapshots: Use tools like `sysstat` to collect performance data. vmstat 1 5

1. **Historical Data:** Analyze trends using tools like `sar`.

   Real-Life Example: An application slows down intermittently. Using `strace`, you discover a specific function call causing delays, allowing for targeted optimization.

Case Studies of Complex Issues

Problem Overview

Real-world examples provide practical insights into troubleshooting complex issues.

Symptoms

- Multi-system failures.
- Intermittent problems requiring advanced techniques.

Solution

1. Break down the problem into smaller components.
2. Use tools like centralized logging and network monitoring for root cause analysis.
3. Apply fixes systematically, testing after each change.

   Real-Life Example: A multi-region cloud architecture experiences outages. Using centralized logs and performance profiling, the issue is traced to a misconfigured load balancer causing regional traffic routing failures.

Lessons Learned from Real-World Problems

Problem Overview

Troubleshooting in complex systems offers lessons for improving future operations.

Symptoms

- Recurring or widespread issues.

Solution

1. Implement proactive monitoring to detect issues earlier.
2. Refine processes based on lessons learned from past failures.
3. Enhance system resilience through redundancy and fault tolerance.

   Real-Life Example: After resolving a distributed database issue, the team sets up robust health checks and alerting mechanisms to prevent future occurrences.

Summary and Glossary

Key Takeaways

- Advanced troubleshooting in multi-system environments requires centralized logging, trace logs, and system snapshots.
- Intermittent issues can be managed with persistent monitoring and detailed logging.
- Case studies provide valuable lessons for refining troubleshooting processes.

Glossary

- **Trace Logs:** Detailed logs tracking function calls and system activities.

- **Centralized Logging:** Aggregation of logs from multiple systems for unified analysis.
- **System Snapshots:** Captures of system states for diagnosing performance or stability issues.
- **Distributed Systems:** Systems with components spread across multiple machines or regions, working as a cohesive unit.
  Note: Effective advanced troubleshooting ensures minimal downtime and enhances system reliability in complex environments.